Contemporary Australian Studies

Literature, History, Film and Media Studies in a Globalizing Age

Edited by
Yasue ARIMITSU and Yuga SUZUKI

Otowa-Shobo Tsurumi-Shoten

Contemporary Australian Studies
Literature, History, Film and Media Studies
in a Globalizing Age

Copyright © 2016
by Yasue ARIMITSU and Yuga SUZUKI

All rights reserved

ISBN978-4-7553-0292-3

Acknowledgement

This book is published on the basis of the "International Symposium" held at Doshisha University in 2012, which all the authors attended. The Symposium was partly subsidised by Doshisha University. We would like to express our gratitude to Doshisha University and all the contributors to this book.

We would also like to express our great appreciation to the Australia Japan Foundation (AJF), an organization of the Australian Government, who subsidised this publication and supported our project. Without their support, this publication would not have been realized. We would also like to congratulate AJF on the 40th Anniversary of its establishment.

We finally wish to thank the publisher, Mr Takashi Yamaguchi of Otowa-Shobo Tsurumi-Shoten, for his great assistance and patience in publishing this book.

Introduction

The purpose of publishing the book, *Contemporary Australian Studies: Literature, History, Film and Media Studies in a Globalizing Age*, is to exchange information about Australian studies among scholars who specialize in literature, history, film and media studies and join forces with one another in our research. The key words of the book are: "multiculturalism," "globalization," and "transformation." Under the policy of multiculturalism in Australia, a drastic transformation in various areas has been observed and this transformation corresponds to the transformation of continuing worldwide globalization.

In this book, we intend to consider the issues of "multiculturalism" and "globalization" and discuss them from interdisciplinary viewpoints such as literature, history, and film and media studies. We also intend to trace different and multiple views of the issues according to geographical areas as we invite authors from five different countries: Kate Darian-Smith (Australia), Guanglin Wang (China), Shiao-Ying Shen (Taiwan), Yeon Lee (Korea) and Yuga Suzuki and Yasue Arimitsu (Japan).

Kate Darian-Smith introduces a history of Australian television, focusing on how multicultural television programs developed in the multicultural society of Australia along with its multicultural policy. Shiao-Ying Shen introduces female storytellers of Australia and New Zealand and indicates how they tackle multiculturalism and globalization in their works from gender minority viewpoints. Yeon Lee and Yuga Suzuki introduce the processes of how Korean and Japanese societies are changing from mono-cultural to multicultural societies, and argue that the media in both countries is playing a great role in these processes.

Guanglin Wang discusses the issue of translation of Australian literary works into Chinese. He argues that a writer with a multicultural background has a different sense of memory and past, and, therefore, the sense of identity in literature is undergoing transformation in the multicultural and globalizing world. Yasue Arimitsu selected Australian literary works and argues that, in a multicultural society, it becomes very difficult to specify the authors' ethnic, cultural, and sometimes national identities from their literary works, and by analysing a work written by a writer from a multicultural background, shows that, therefore, literary identity is being transformed.

The book thus reflects multicultural and global viewpoints not just from the conventional dual perspectives such as between Japan and Australia, China and Australia, or the West and the East, and deepens our understanding of the concepts of "multiculturalism" and "globalization" and attempts to form a more comprehensive view of the future. I would like to introduce the articles briefly with the hope that, by reading this book, readers will be able to grasp a future view of multiculturalism and globalization, and the transformation of cultural, ethnic, and literary identities.

Guanglin WANG wrote about translating the contemporary Australian writer, Brian Castro's *Shanghai Dancing* (2003). Wang argues, with reference to Walter Benjamin's "The Task of the Translator," that the translation of Castro's *Shanghai Dancing* into Chinese creates a "theoretical problem" which is related to reading and cognitive functions. Wang points out that this problem occurs not between two European tongues, but between an encompassing East/West axis, and mutates historical models which appear to go beyond post-colonial narrative in today's global world. As a result, Wang observes that Benjamin's theory is no longer appropriate for translating Castro's work from English into Chinese, which has a completely different language structure as well as function from the original English.

Wang then contends that Castro's novel is an example of a new sense of history and identity of an ethnic writer in a multicultural and globalizing age, and translating this novel provides a different theory of translation. Wang thus attempts to grasp the change in the notion of identity and history, and indicate the loss of authentic origin in writing novels, and even the changed function of language since the appearance of authors from hybrid backgrounds in this globalizing world. There is no cultural or ethnic authenticity or identity when cultural or ethnic immersion occurs. Wang attempts to present another dimension of the meaning of language, identity and history.

Shiao-Ying SHEN's paper introduces six female storytellers from Down Under and illustrates how they cope with the issues of globalization in their art works. Shen claims that two playwrights, Alma De Groen and Hannie Rayson, tackle globalization in the form of corporatization of intellectual institutions, and this manifests itself through the all-encompassing force of the north, particularly through English tales and dramatic plots from the northern hemisphere, and therefore, deletes the narratives from the south.

Shen argues that the visual artist Tracey Moffatt presents her works in a different maneuvering of the global-multicultural dynamic, and makes effective use of a global style to empower her unveiling of

Australian stories. Shen focuses on Moffatt's photographs which show the mixing of white, Chinese, and Aboriginal presence, and remarks that Moffatt suggested the possibility of reconciliation even before the idea became state policy.

Shen considers Jane Campion, a female filmmaker, who produced the popular film *The Piano*, set in New Zealand. She uses the wild landscape of New Zealand for her film, but she goes beyond the local to make it universal. Sue Brooks, in her film *Japanese Story*, tells an Australian story. The film needs the shock of the Other, a foreigner, and in so doing the Japanese male is feminized so as to bring out qualities in the Australian female. Clara Law is another film maker from Hong Kong who deals with the fear of displacement and an ambivalent sense of identity. Her documentary, *Letters to Ali*, traces a journey to visit a young Afghan asylum seeker, freeing Law from being Chinese and uprooting her own self identity. Through making films, she finds a new sense of the filmic, and manifests home as a form of film act. For her, filming is home, her own identity.

Yasue ARIMITSU deals with the issues of subjectivity and otherness in literature in the globalizing age. She argues that literature in a multicultural Australia has been transforming from the conventional literature which was based on a nation with one culture, one ethnicity and one language. Literary works written in a multicultural society make it difficult for readers to identify their authors' national, cultural, and ethnic identities as the authors often cross those borders. Arimitsu introduces the cases of B. Wongar and Helen Demidenko, which caused sensations in the 1970s and 1980s, when multiculturalism started and continued to penetrate Australia. In both cases, the authors crossed ethnic borders for their own political reasons, although they still remained in the binary postcolonial framework of the colonizer and the colonized, or the mainstream and the periphery.

However, in the 2000s, the trend changed. In his collected short stories, Nam Le creates different characters whose identities are different from his own. In this, the author attempts not simply to cross national, ethnic, and cultural borders, but to transcend them. He even attempts to remove his own national, ethnic, and cultural identity as if he were removing his own subjectivity. The case of Nam Le's collected short stories shows one example of the transformation of modern literature in a globalizing age. In this work, Nam Le removes his subjectivity and at the same time, he deconstructs the binary framework of subject and other.

Kate DARIAN-SMITH discusses how Australian television developed in the 1950s, through the 1970s, and up until the late twentieth century when newer media and communication technologies were introduced. When television appeared in 1956, it did not yet represent Australian ethnic diversity, as personalities and actors appearing in locally produced television dramas were generally limited to Anglo-Australians. However, television played a very important role for immigrants in settling into their new country, getting to know the Australian way of life and language, and as the source of a wide range of other information. Darian-Smith discusses the cases of Italian and Greek immigrants, showing how important television was for them to learn English, particularly for children. For the children of migrants, television was not only entertainment but also a benevolent tool for teaching them local rituals and habits.

Darian-Smith argues that television also served as a bridge between Australia and the wider world in the 1950s and 1960s. It played a unique role in providing insight into the histories and cultures of Asia such as Japan and China. She takes up *The Samurai* series using American-accented English which introduced a samurai warrior in eighteenth-century Japan to the Australian audience. She also argues that the American television series *Kung Fu* provided the Australian audience with images of China and its culture. She adds that in the 1990s, SBS television, which purchased many programs from overseas including Europe and Asia, and, after the 2000s, the changes in media technologies and Australia's changing population, where in many cases non-English languages are spoken at home, have meant that there are new ways for diasporic communities to interact with their home and host countries by both using and bypassing conventional television.

Yeon LEE writes about multiculturalism in Korea. Lee argues that the Korean society is now transforming from a traditional mono-ethnic society into a multicultural society, and that the media plays a great role in integrating that multicultural society. Korea started to accept immigrants from overseas when it hosted the 2002 World Cup and then began to encourage international marriage and also accept the migration of foreign workers as well as international students. This has been a great influence on Korean society. Lee argues that traditional Korean society was based on Confucianism which teaches people to respect their ancestors and that Korean people tended to be biased against foreign or multi-ethnic people, but since the society has become multicultural, and foreigners or multi-ethnic Koreans have increased, the prejudice against them is decreasing as they attempt to assimilate into Korean society.

Lee argues that media played an important role in communications between Koreans and immigrants; particularly television, radio, newspapers, and magazines provide a lot of information about the values of the host society, although the Internet requires caution and prudence. The Korean government supports immigrants by integrating them into the multicultural society. Lee, by giving some examples of cultural differences, shows that Korean people are now accepting people with different cultures or languages and concludes that Korea is now becoming multicultural alongside those representative multicultural nations such as the United States, Canada, and Australia.

Yuga SUZUKI writes about the Japanese media in relation to that of multicultural Australia. The Japanese government does not advocate multiculturalism, but in reality, there are a considerable number of immigrants in Japan. Suzuki explains the historical process of how foreigners, particularly Chinese and Koreans, came to Japan from the Edo period, until the present time when Japanese economic growth brought more foreigners with a variety of national and cultural backgrounds to Japan. Along with these movements, Suzuki focuses on the role of media such as television, radio, newspapers, and magazines, and analyzes the relationship between media and language ability of non-Japanese immigrants.

Suzuki examines Japanese multicultural media referring to the Australian Special Broadcasting Service (SBS) which was established as a public body of Australian multiculturalism. Suzuki argues that SBS has played an important role in the multicultural society of Australia, but in Japan, this service has both merits and demerits. Immigrants who use multicultural media are able to obtain information through their own languages, but on the other hand, they are enclosed in their own world without assimilating to Japanese society, culture, and lifestyle. Suzuki also points out political aspects of the media. Residents from North Korea or China sometimes use the Japanese media in order to express their political views because freedom of expression is protected in Japan, and this is another issue which needs to be further researched.

Yasue Arimitsu

Contents

Acknowledgements iii

Introduction v

Guanglin WANG

Translating Fragments:
On the Sino-Anglo "Convolutes" in Brian Castro's *Shanghai Dancing* 1

Shiao-Ying SHEN

Facing the Global by Way of the Multicultural:
A Look into Antipodean Women Storytellers 39

Yasue ARIMITSU

"Subjectivity" and "Otherness" in Australian Literature 67

Kate DARIAN-SMITH

Expanding Horizons:
Australian Television and Globalization in the 1950s–1970s 95

Yeon LEE

Multiculturalism and Media in Korean Society 121

Yuga SUZUKI

Japanese Media and Multicultural Society 133

Contributors 149

Translating Fragments:
On the Sino-Anglo "Convolutes" in Brian Castro's *Shanghai Dancing*

Guanglin WANG
Shanghai University of International Business and Economics, China

In 'The Task of the Translator' (1923), a text used as introduction to his translation of Baudelaire's Tableaux Parisiens, Walter Benjamin famously shifts the problem of translation against the Western mimetic premise of translation's aim (reproduction, copying). That is, from a concern with the original being reproduced, or any monolinguism being given priority, he posits an occurrence "between" languages—and references a "greater language" of which any two (say, original French, translational German) are fragments. It is not always noted (the idioms Benjamin uses involve head fakes of sorts, traditions cited and emptied at once) that with this he closes the "modernist" model of translation. This topos of "translation" is at once spawned as a theoretical problem that absorbs reading, cognitive functions, and language itself as what is, finally, not "human," opening on to what one might call a 21st century problematic—one present, say, in his *Theses on the Philosophy of History*, when what is mocked as an "angel of history" (one we personify to provide a mock messianic narrative) gives way to what is called, in climactic metaphors, a "storm." Benjamin's text stumbles into a very different logic which, briefly, I would like to re-orient and apply to what

I would call a 21st century writing, consciously "Benjaminian," in Brian Castro's Shanghai Dancing—a writing, too, which occurs at the crease not between two European tongues, but between an encompassing East/West axis, between a Chinese writing that appears positioned outside of alphabeticism, close to the logics of "image," and a sense of non-linear time and mutating historical models that appear to rupture the post-colonial narrative, today's "global" world inherits yet suddenly exceeds—as the human itself is posed not as a national but a species question, one that delivers us to the very unsatisfying (and perhaps regressive) promises of trans-human or post-human discourse.

If Walter Benjamin's translational hypothesis turns, often, to cities as its allegorical palimpsest, not only Naples, or Moscow, or Marseilles, but Paris most centrally (in the *Arcades Project*), where it is as if "read" as the prehistorial template of modernity, what would one say of the "Paris of the East," of a "Shanghai" that becomes this tele-urban point of transition, in which global languages and memory systems are in critical reconfiguration? Whatever would be called "Shanghai" would appear, perhaps, the locus of a different logic of the fragment than one which, in the "angelic" modernism which Benjamin discretely destroys, references itself back to being a fragment of an original whole, a "vessel" perhaps. What is a fragment that does not index itself to what it is a fragment of, or in which the ruin returns as a citational premise—as prolix and uncontainably launched as Shanghai's notorious skyline or the zombie-business district of a conjured Pudong it idyllically looks out over.

Benjamin's argument is that:

> Translation thus ultimately serves the purpose of expressing the central reciprocal relationship between languages. It cannot

possibly reveal or establish this hidden relationship itself; but it can represent it by realizing it in embryonic or intensive form. This representation of hidden significance through an embryonic attempt at making it visible is of so singular a nature that it is rarely met with in the sphere of nonlinguistic life.

(Benjamin, 72)

In this passage, neither literary works nor their readers should be confined to monolingualism. The translator's "task" (*Aufgabe*) is to liberate any appearance of a mono-language imprisoned in literary works. For Benjamin, translation already marks a survival and an afterlife of an original text, and this *life-death* metaphor adds an important dimension as well to intra-cultural communication on the experiential level today. It is, most simply, the experience of the linguistic migrant.

Benjamin relinquishes the core notion of faithfulness to an *original* that, as noted, was always emphasized in Western mimetic tradition. When we encounter the trope of the vessel which suggests wholeness and is borrowed from Kaballalist thought, we may not notice that said *vessel* does not do what it implies at first. It does not carry any content (as a vessel of transport would suggest), and it is not to be pieced together again by the *fragments* referenced after the fact as its shattered shards. The Kabbalistic trope of *fragments of the vessel* suggests a unity-in-diversity while ignoring that the *whole* never arrives, was never given (it is not the original text being translated, say) and is retro-projected from the position of the fragment—which now is so defined without being a *fragment of* . . . :

Fragments of a vessel which are to be glued together must

match one another in the smallest details, although they need not be like one another. In the same way a translation, instead of resembling the meaning of the original, must lovingly and in detail incorporate the original's mode of signification, thus making both the original and the translation recognizable as fragments of a greater language, just as fragments are part of a vessel. (Benjamin, 78)

What is this "greater language," enigmatic and debated by critics? Does it combine different languages into a coherent whole, or does it suggest something else? Any so-called "greater language" is not, after all, some Platonic zone of pure meaning: what Benjamin calls "pure language [*reine Sprache*]" references something like a "pure" *materiality without meaning* at all, which languages and mnemonic technologies necessarily share (think of marks, or sound before any letteration, any pictogram, any network of sounds).

Throughout both modernism and postmodernism, translation—which requires close reading *and* an understanding of cultures—has become an interdisciplinary problem influenced by many different fields. It takes as its premise a cultural mosaic with "a combination of diverse elements forming a more or less coherent whole," yet calls to attention the otherness of linguistic and cultural forms.

I.

Translators have long been baffled by the debate between faithfulness to an original and betrayal, which the Western mimetic tradition perpetuates in its dedication to the figure of the copy, or the *eidos*. But the process is lived perpetually, much as it (translation) mimes in Benjamin a problem that adheres to reading, to image as such, to "cinema," or finally, to what he terms "materialistic historiography." For migrants in the age of globalization, conceptions of translation assume a new role as the latter are associated with their bafflement and the mainstream debates of their identity. Rather than regard *translation* as static or finite, one should see translation as an element in networks of mobility, which can meet and interact with each other at any given moment, and the cultures in question take the form of global hybrids. The exercise of translating, according to Cronin, is central to the identity of the immigrant. As he notes:

> The condition of the migrant is the condition of the translated being. He or she moves from a source language and culture to a target language and culture so that translation takes place both in the physical sense of movement or displacement and in the symbolic sense of the shift from one way of speaking, writing about and interpreting the world to another. (Cronin, 45)

Translators have long agreed that a good translator seems like a Jack of all trades, as he or she must have a broad range of knowledge and understand different cultural and linguistic values. How much of the foreign or of the other should the translator maintain? How much of the foreign or the other should the translator erase to make the text more accessible to the target reader? And in what way should a translator piece together the fragments of the broken vessel, especially in this age of globalization where the clash of civilizations still rings. By putting translation in the context of diasporic movement, Cronin maintains that all translators are cultural cosmopolitans, in that going to the other text, the other language, the other culture, involves that initial journey away from the location of one's birth, language, and upbringing. Even if one is translating into the foreign language as a target language, there is still the element of displacement, as the translator moves from the native language to the other language. Translation therefore creates a "dialogical self" in advance, an identity that can be viewed in different perspectives.

We can review why the pragmatics of translation remains theoretically pregnant and interminably suggestive, today, when the global era, as it were, positions not just French and German adjacent to one another (Benjamin's case with Baudelaire), but more massively Asian pictographics and alphabeticist monotheisms as forms a writing, technologies of memory—and specifically, global English and Chinese, including an unreadability the latter maintains to the former. (I will examine this gap, in a moment, in *Shanghai Dancing*.) If the fragments of the vessel include original and translation, then there is no whole "vessel" to ever get back too or restore, and the fragments never to re-assemble in place nor, finally, can they. And this is why the logic of translation, including Benjamin's, takes on a different shading in 21st century post-global contexts of exchange and commerce.

Etymologically the term translation—*trans* (across) and *latus* (to carry)—can be equated with a transportation of meaning and a displacement. In Benjamin's German it is *Ueber-setzung*, a carrying-over that, nonetheless, may also go hyper as if while staying in place—thus, its affinity with *meta-phorein* as such, the transit and transport of figurative language. Yet this transport is not a one-directional effort, carrying one language or culture into another, but rather a dialogic one in which social and historical elements are interspersed. At the same time, it hints at what Benjamin calls a "one-way street" elsewhere—a movement as if away from individual or national appropriations, away from proper meaning, from any phantom of a "home," from monolinguisms at all.

Translation does not provide a universal criterion for the rendition of a culturally-loaded semantic text, but it does provide a chance for a creative negotiation of differences, wherein exchanges of cultures can be affected, cultural chasms breached. It is a philosophical domain, yet entirely practical too—at once cognitive and linguistic. For Benjamin, the original and its translation are both "recognizable as the fragments of a greater language, just as fragments are parts of a vessel" (Benjamin, 78). This greater language, or "pure language," however debatable as to its existence or figural sense, is the means by which the translator can be released from a language which is under the spell of another, starting with her or his *own*. It is not the original of which the translation is a fragment, both are fragments of a vessel that was never apprehended before it would have been shattered. Of course, the translator is alert to "historical hauntings" in conveying meanings of a culturally-loaded foreign text (Bermann and Wood, 6). The translation marks (and performs) a survival of the texts; without translation, the so-called original will die; the translation reinterprets the original for different audiences in different contexts.

The trope of the broken vessel implies a *fragmentariness* in the absence of the (unbroken) vessel, with its promise at least of containment (an urn), purveyance (a vessel in transit). In *Fragments of Modernity: Theories of Modernity in the Work of Simmel, Kracauer, and Benjamin* (1988), David Frisby analyzes the common thread shared by Simmel,

Kracauer, and Benjamin, that is, the fragmentary, fugitive, transient and contingent character of experience as portrayed by Baudelaire. If Frisby thinks that Benjamin is the most difficult to understand, here, it may have something to do with the fragmentary, its prestige in Benjamin and the latter's practice of it—angling against the apothegms of Nietzsche as a style. Benjamin's *Passagenwerk* or *Arcades Project* is actually a collection of organized fragments using the city life of Paris in the 19th century as its template. Elsewhere in Benjamin "cities" acquire the import of palimpsests to be read, verbal archeographies. *The Arcades Project*, which would be posthumously edited and never given a completed form, takes this Paris as the blueprint of the modern prehistory—a role that Shanghai will assume, differently, in Brian Castro's writing.

Benjamin maintains the dream-like narration of the city life. To accept the reality of this world is to accept the dream world of modernity which turns the real world into a nightmare. The *arcade*, a sequence of passages, textual and transportive, mimes the labyrinth of the modern metropolis. The idler also indulges his desire to idle, in temporal eddies. The archival arcade, the city and the underground world—in Paris, the catacombs or the unconscious of the photograph—are excavated by Benjamin's writing project. The 19th-century Paris, like the stone embedded in the forest, would be a ruin as if exposed to light, except that for Benjamin, "light" would itself be the product of letters ("illuminations"). The fragments, the dialectical images, the concept of prehistory, the critique of the historical consciousness, cinema, awakening, "materialistic historiography," collectors and the idlers are all points of articulation in Benjamin's project that in turn mutate into allegorical logics. By allegorical we do not mean some reflexive performance by the text marking its own scene of production—that is, a still representational notion—but something else, something performative, that negates and alters the premises out of which a certain "present" had been projected or artificed. These are mutating centers of the *Arcades Project* of Benjamin. For Benjamin, it is the *fragments* that keep the channel for the totality, rather than the totality project unto the fragments.

The Arcades Project "invites raiding rather than reading. . . . One starts from the Exposes, from the sketches, from the list of convolutes, from the index, from the cross-references, the notes and bibliography. One dives in rather than swims through" (Buse, vii). Ambitious as the project is (1074 sheets), as a "book" it consists of thirty-six convolutes, as they are called—with 26 convolutes with upper case letters from A to Z, and 10 convolutes of lower case letters. They are laced with fleeting images, quotations, notes, or citations dotted here and there, and all are related to nineteenth century Paris. For instance, "Convolute B is 'Fashion,' D 'Boredom, eternal return,' M 'The Flâneur,' d 'Literary history, Hugo,' and m 'Idleness.' The shortest one, 'Reproduction technology, lithography,' takes up only two pages, while the longest, 'Baudelaire.' extends to 160" (Buse, 2–3), and "Among the many literary encounters of the *Arcades Project*, Baudelaire figures most prominently. In Baudelaire Benjamin found the archetypal *flâneur* strolling through the arcades in decline. The term *flâneur* was coined around 1806 and refers to an individual whose state of heightened individuality and interiority spurs him to romantic journeying in the infinity of the self. In the work of Baudelaire it got another meaning, becoming associated with the notion of stimuli. The *flâneur* is open to stimuli and walks the streets of the modern city at a slow and leisurely pace, an observer and recorder of modernity, an archetypal modern subject, passive and open, restrained and appreciative, a customer of the world. . . . The *flâneur* is searching, at least, if in a superficial and random way" (Buse, 4).

III.

Brian Castro's understanding of a literary text continues the tradition of modernism. Although critics tend to view Castro with a postmodernist stance, Castro himself never acknowledges that, rather he would accept a high modernist labeling. In her close analysis of the author's published novels, *Brian Castro's fiction: the seductive play of language* (2008), Bernadette Brennan links Castro with Patrick White because Castro is considered an "intellectual, deeply ironic, modernist writer" (Brennan, 1). In a large sense, Castro can be situated in a wider European context of modernist writings, works by Marcel Proust, Franz Kafka, Walter Benjamin, Virginia Woolf, Thomas Mann, James Joyce, Gustav Flaubert, Vladimir Nabokov, W. G. Sebald (Brennan, 2)[1]. In following the modernist tradition of Benjamin, Castro tries to link a work of art with history, the conscious representation with the unconscious, and fragments with the whole, as he claims that "Writing knows no boundaries. Its metaphors, its translations, are part of a migratory process, birds of passage, which wing from the subliminal to the page, leaving their signs for the reader. Meanwhile the writer stands a little to the side, shooting arrows into the wind, with an expression of alarmed uncertainty as the traces disappear into the eternal roar of society's unconscious" (Castro 1999, 35).

In Brian Castro's *Shanghai Dancing*, an inviting "raiding rather than reading" autobiographical fiction, we feel the trope of the broken vessel, or the vessel in fragments, which leaves us in a dilemma as to whether to restore the wholeness of this vessel, or to display the fragments simply as it is. As is normal with the reader, we would love to piece together the fragments from the novel, and try to dig, through history and memory, the sense of history and identity of an ethnic writer. As an autobiographical novel, the author tries to restore, in intentional fragmentation and memories, the wholeness of the story and re-create the missing parts. In the novel we can feel the efforts of translation to piece together a family history out of the fragments of memory. Castro's work, a tour de force that touches a variety of disciplines such as philosophy, comparative literature, film studies, art history, urban studies, and history, can be read as a reconfiguration of Benjaminian traces (whose specific influence on Castro is explicit).

In *Shanghai Dancing*, we witness a modern Portuguese *flâneur* (Castro, 396) as represented by Antonio Castro seeking adventures in Shanghai—in which an "Arcades" effect is applied to this different, sino-anglo "Paris of the East," which names also a linguistic and archival non-site (displacing Rome, for Freud, or Paris, for Benjamin). As the "vessel" that is not aside from fragments, which has no "home" (or exile from which to return), a more determined, amodernist Benjaminian logic emerges—the "one-way street" which the modernist, Marxian, theological, and deconstructive "Benjamins" appear regressive before today. In Antonio Castro we can sense not only a history of the Castro family, but also a prehistory of the "modern" world. The author draws upon a unique reservoir of newspapers, magazines, documents, pillow books, photographs and illustrations to trace the origin and the rise and fall of his family. Spatially the author takes us through Shanghai, Australia, Hong Kong Macau, Japan, Portugal, Spain and England, temporally the author takes us across 17th century and 20th century, and linguistically the author shifts between English, French, Spanish, Portuguese, and

Cantonese, representing the linguistic code-switching and challenges the traditional monolingual linear way of narration. Delving deep into the world of cabarets, nightclubs, and elite ballrooms that are a hallmark of Shanghai modernity in the 1920s and 1930s, the novel assesses how a Portuguese *flâneur* gets involved in a metropolitan city of Shanghai where different cultures are converged, and, accompanying the sense of modernity, the readers follow the descriptions of colonialism and modernity, jazz-band and entertainments, sexuality and modern Chinese national identity formation. The secret, the opium, the silent mother, the arrogant and uninhibited father, the smart sister, the liar, the missionary, the gambler, the lover, and the orphan, all these are called into Castro's writing. Antonia Antonio Castro bears the traits of the Baudelairean *flâneur* as elaborated in the *Arcades Project*. He sometimes falls into a dream, and sometimes stays awake, shifting between the two worlds:

> My father is dozing. I put the cigar on the Lazy Susan in front of him. On the shelf beneath, his decanter of Portuguese port filters the afternoon light ruby-red; trembles from the earthquake of his snoring and shaking. His practiced fingers flip and twitch over an old guidebook in his lap: *A Complete Look at Shanghai Philandering*. Like all dreams, there is always a precise map of the location, and I can see the streets of Shanghai . . . his *Passagenwerk* . . . unfurl before his drooping glasses like a divine emanation. (255)

In the above the *Arcades Project* is openly cited, and considered a "divine emanation." Antonia Antonio Castro seems to indulge in dreams, be claimed by memory or the past, like any reproduction machine or technology (like any writing) but he is also trying to seize the day, if we may invoke the carpe diem to trope what Benjamin ends up calling by a number of ghosted terms (blasting, Now-time), since said "now" can only be seized as its own afterlife, and as where "life" itself emerges as such. He is split between the two worlds. Brian Castro, in his essay "Bridging Cultural Concept," manifests that "writing is a 'schizoid process'" (cited in Ommundsen, 154), implying that a writer is split into different worlds in different identities. In this autographical writing, Castro follows *The Arcades Project* by beginning each chapter with an upper-case alphabet, but the alphabets do not follow in a linear way, with for example the second chapter W(inter) follows the first chapter A, and takes 28 pages, while A takes only a little more than one page. This prioritization of the alphabet and its Western legacies, from monotheism through technological conquest, resonates. Brian Castro would later confide that this novel's composition was influenced by the Chinese Writer Han Shaogong's *A Dictionary of Maqiao*, but the *Arcades Project* influence is felt more. The novel is quite encyclopedic in that it begins with A and ends with Z, hoping to embrace not a personal history, but a dictionary of cultures. In fact, Shanghai Dancing is built through a chain of chapters, most of which are short and fragmentary, like Benjaminian "snapshots." Form is shaped to serve content, or more accurately, "content" is—like cultural identity—a mimetic misnomer, the contract of a blind system of historical proprietary (monolingual) meanings, and "form" perhaps names what remains, what Benjamin again, in the essay on translation, celebrated as a language without "meaning." Different melodic lines are put in play, under the (invariably Nietzschean) rubric of the dance, and as the narrative builds these begin to interact, overlapping and intersecting, to generate what cannot be contained by as any sum of supposed parts. Fragments re-center, coalesce, dissolve, others flash up—as on a dancefloor, even as the figure of dancing draws on invariably to feet, footprints, stampings out, the material trace at its most irreducible (Benjamin's "pure language"?). This intertextual rendition corresponds to Barthes's argument that "The text is a tissue of quotations drawn from the innumerable centers of culture . . . (the author's) only power is to mix writings, to counter the ones with the others, in such a way as never to rest on any one of them" (Bassnett and Lefevere, 27).

According to Benjamin, history never suggests stasis; rather, it signifies flux, a precise present moment that stands in relation to an event or object from the past. Allegory captures the difference between what historical events once meant and what they mean now: the space that was once a sacred religious site, a temple in the past, in the present stands as an assemblage of fragments open to many possible significations. For Benjamin historical texts (and all written forms) are present allegorical representations of past events. Revolutionary veterans in the early nation were, like Benjamin's ruins, both embodiments of decrepitude and destitution and open signifiers for what the Revolution might represent in historical texts.

As a fictional autobiography, *Shanghai Dancing* traces the family history of the Castros from the narrator Antonio's initiation into fragmented memory talk of the grandparents who cross the borders of Europe and came to Shanghai to seek their fortune, to the narrator's personal experience in Shanghai and his recognition by others and what it means to be an "I" in the multicultural world. The narrator, in translating his multiple experiences, often gets stuck in linguistic maneuvers, to explain to others who he is, often in a way reminiscent of traumatic past.

> At the moment I am preoccupied with having to speak to others in a voice that is not mine . . . I find myself addressing the past and all its objet trouvés, all spiraling and revolving and emitting circular noises. The subject of the seminar was: *The Limitations of Translation*. . . . I was speaking about Chinese voices, about how to translate distress. Does trauma feed invention instead of truth? (Castro 2003, 323)

For ethnic writers, trauma feeds imagination instead of truth because they have come across issues of cultural identity, of racism that is imposed upon the ethnic minority in a multicultural world, and this cultural identity and recognition in the mainstream society gives much pain to the writer. But we see where Castro finds it necessary to invert this form of repetitive enslavement, and the myths of subjectivity which it enforces under the illusion of political positioning. In a diary as recorded at 11:45 a.m., 29, August, 1991, Castro experiences despair, suffering, fear, and loathing. He thought he was soon to be dead (Castro 2008, 112). This alienation, this mimic way of life-death compels a multiplex of cultural perspectives, each convoluted as embedded in serially fragmented networks. And it compels a rethinking of the penal origins of white settlement, as he later observes: "I would like to suggest that this is what the hybrid has to offer: the time of reflection which provokes vision out of the trauma of being torn. Without losing sight of the dual propensities of melancholy for paralysis and for productive creativity, the hybrid's mourning for the loss of authenticity originally encourages the subject to hide inside his or her wound. From this, creativity is coerced" (Castro 2008, 121). The wound both is inescapable, laced in the language and literary flux of the Anglo multiverse, etched into the global matrix as initiating scar and trap—yet resisted as the anchor of identification. Castro, with Benjamin, slips the closure of 20th century identity fetishization at the point of immersion, and does so as the unreadable but primordial Chinese pictogram and its metonymic echo, the photograph, all but digitalized, disarticulates the Western algorithms of a death drive that has spawned, today, the species perspective of an "anthropocene" era.

From the beginning, the narrator tries to translate the sense of the term *Shanghai Dancing*, but the readers experience disorientation and fragmentation as the effect of it as a performative ("dancing") overrides interpretation heard as hermeneutic production of proper meanings. The dancing of feet—the material traces of a "greater language" defined as without mere meaning—assert their priority over the head, invert the body and take the position of the *capo*, eye, or cognitive center (a Western imposition). The title suggests at the same time what is unclosed, prolific, inauthentic, without referential anchor, as the ambiguous fame of Shanghai, faux "Paris of the East," reverberates in association with harlotry, mimicry, absorption: since English resides over a more primary language which defines (and names) Shanghai, even Chinese is here to be understood as not "originary," an organization of marks. There is, for instance, the "Shanghai dancing" which translates as attainment of disorientation and instability, and there is that, as in navy slang, which stands for venereal disease—which will be later associated in the work with his father's syphilis. There is also a "Shanghai dancing" which in Australasian slang means catapult, and will be connected with Marbles, a character whom Antonio later suspects of being his half-brother. He often stays on the roof of the building of Antonio's school, sometimes firing slingshot pellets across at the students. Yet the true identity of

Marbles is never revealed, especially the relationship between Marbles's death and his own exile to Australia. "I have a strong suspicion that everything my father left, has been left to this dark shadow. That was the beginning of my breakdown; the hallucination of phantom brothers; the affliction of marbles"(Castro, 29). He cannot be sure of any of this. But a line has been cast, a central part of the melody has been laid down, and he will keep coming back to it throughout the novel. The *dancing*—of the name, place, history, writing of "Shanghai," no longer arcade but perhaps digital mall—redistributes the logic of the flâneur.

In *Shanghai Dancing*, we can see the creation out of a deconstruction of the traditional authoritative sense of biography, the authorized narration of (a) life, for in this fictional family biography, the reader is led into a labyrinth renavigating the backlooping artifices of both time and space. This geographical displacement compels the text to move across Shanghai, Macau, Hong Kong, and other Asian and European *cities*. The "novel houses and is housed by the telepolis. The novel traces back through time channel to the empires overlapping across the world, shuffling between 17th century Brazil, Goa, Nagasaki, the Philippines, Liverpool, Paris, and the period of handover of Hong Kong to China in 1997, and the life in contemporary Australia. In "Auto/biography," an essay later collected in his essay collection, *Looking for Estrelliata*, Castro shows his interest in how the documents of one's life are distilled and sedimented, "not in terms of fact or fiction, but in terms of narrative and memory" (Castro 1999, 101). He is skeptical of the coherent life writing as he grows up in different cultural background and speaks different languages. The essayistic writing melds the auto-biographizations of nationalism, life, self, writing. In a lecture delivered at Shanghai Library Castro alludes in his early days to his obsession with the girl he calls Estrellita, who he thinks stimulates him into writing when he feels depressed, and this Estrellita appears in his early novel *Pomeroy* as well as the embodiment of a love lost. He said she is a cousin, but Estrellita functions more as a symbol, a symbol of his love for the writing, a symbol of his quest for the loss, for his desire to be recognized. He is indulged in his dream world, mixing genre, categories, facts and fiction. In *Shanghai Dancing*, his efforts of mixing are conveyed through cultural differences represented by his father and his mother respectively. Talking of his father, he observed: "I think he was a liar. Most of his sides of the family were liars. But then you could never say that categorically because every now and again you would come up against the truth . . . The truth-appeasers were on my mother's side. They never said anything about themselves . . . but on my father's side . . . full-scale fabrications" (Castro 2003, 32).

The vignettes in *Shanghai Dancing* would have been haunting Castro for years. He had to write them. The challenge was to seek where words and grammar could be pushed beyond their categorial limits, and it would take ten years for the novel to be published, forming in turn an event of the "life," generated by the writing. Though based on biography, the work is inseparable from that of memory, which to an ethnic writer is closely connected with his background or origins—even as a writing that seeks to divest itself of a (lying) genealogy. Memory is easily distorted over time, and therefore the script of an ethnic writer marks a process of generating memory and translating it into something else. This translation process is both an inscription, and a transformation of tradition. On one side of the Castro family, there was predominantly Portuguese influence, with its affection for empire, and indulgence, while on the other there was a fusion of "British stiff upper lip and Chinese self-effacement" (Castro 2003, 243). At school in Hong Kong, he experienced great diversity as the children from different national background gather together, but he was forced by his father to board a plane for Australia where what he saw was but mono-cultural in comparison with his life in Hong Kong. The early years in Australia were torture for Castro, as he recalled later: "I knew I was perceived as unnatural. I was forced almost immediately toward definition. . . . Furthermore, as a 'hybrid' (as much as I detest this agricultural terminology) I was never going to be valorized as 'authentically' anything" (Castro 1998, 10). But in *Shanghai Dancing* we encounter the hybridity where the authentic are mixed with (and necessarily as) fabrications. In the "fiction" we find traces of this family. His father was born in Shanghai, and his grandfather came very early to Shanghai to seek his fortune. His maternal grandfather Virgil married his grandmother, a lady from Liverpool. They went back to Liverpool where Virgil studied surgery. Later they came back to China, and in Hong Kong they grew steadily apart. After her death the grandmother was taken back to Liverpool to be buried, but no longer with Virgil. Instead, she had spent the last years of her life with another product of empire, Mr Auberon Untebele, her Nigerian friend who reads Franz Fanon. One of Antonio's many tasks is to accompany Untebele's body to Liverpool, where his ashes would be spread over Dora's grave. On his father's side there were boisterous stories. Many of his strongest memories are of his father at the piano, with uncles and cousins sitting on the veranda of the home in Hong Kong, telling tales of the Portuguese side of the family. There is the combination of Jewish and Catholic elements here, the Jewish great grandfather and the Catholic great grandmother, a *conversos*. The great grandfather comes to Shanghai in the nineteenth century, along with the other Sephardic Jews who were to make such an impact in the colonial ports of the British empire, especially Bombay and Shanghai. These were people like Sir Victor Sassoon, who built the famous Cathay Hotel, and the Kadoories, all of whom feature in the novel, along with other more infamous Shanghai identities, such as Du Yuesheng. The writing echoes the travel of DNA.

As Antonio imagines the lives of these people through the stories told on the veranda when he was young, each segment begins with a "what if," an "imagine," a "suppose," and a "picture this" to indicate what is going on here. Such is storytelling, but then, of course, the tales people tell themselves shape the way they understand their lives and the ways in which they act in the world. The auto/biography unfolds as Castro tries to make sense of the material he has inherited from the family, a bunch of his father's photographs, some memories and lots of overlapping, contradictory stories. He travels to the various cities where they lived, to Shanghai, Macau, Hong Kong, Liverpool, trying to make these traces come alive, but they always refuse narrative clarity. Narratives are always subject to challenge. There are different versions of events, and different versions of people.

Both of his parents would eventually come to Sydney, but only many years later, when he was an adult. "I knew neither of them," and both felt out of place. Arnaldo arrived in pinstripes and spats, looking a lot like Truman Capote or a Chicago gangster, expecting Sydney to be like Hong Kong. Antonio's mother, Jasmine, is even more dislocated. Alienated by language, she hides behind her 'Chineseness.' Castro devotes some of the tenderest moments in the novel to his depiction of his mother. In Shanghai she used to model for *Levers*, and during the war in Hong Kong it was her ingenuity that kept her daughters and stepdaughters alive during the worst of the Japanese occupation. She danced to forget herself, to distance herself from these memories, but she refused to be touched. "A repression of the body is a repression of memory. My mother is embarrassed to touch, to kiss, to show any emotion that betrays either the code of familiarity or the code of horror" (Castro 2003, 242). It was only later, in Australia, with the onset of Alzheimer's, that her life became easier. The terror of the past disappeared along with her memories.

Castro builds *Shanghai Dancing* through a chain of chapters, most of which are short and fragmentary. Some take the form of a 'Pillow Book,' a private journal "in which to record stray thoughts and impressions; a form of free association called 'following the brush" (Castro 2003, 28). Other chapters pick up one line of the melody and let it run for a while. All these fragmented memories and mixings of genres build up and dismember the body of *Shanghai Dancing*, which vaporizes authority and authenticity. How would one classify what is neither novel, nor travelogue, nor memoir, nor history, nor photography, nor simply a summary or "vessel" of them all? As Antonio remarks towards the end of *Shanghai Dancing*, "I believe it is the rhetoric of autobiography, to conceal as much as to reveal" (Castro 2003, 325). Lurking behind this is Paul de Man's observation about the nature of autobiography: "We assume that life *produces* the autobiography as an act produces its consequences, but can we not suggest, with equal justice, that the autobiographical project may itself produce and determine the life and that whatever the writer *does* is in fact governed by the technical demands of self portraiture and thus determined, in all its aspects, by the resources of his medium?" (De Man, 920)

But the turn to the resources of mediums exceeds that of words. In *Shanghai Dancing*, to make up for the inaccuracy of the memory, the writer resorts to photos and posters. The photos and posters serve as a paratext, a "threshold . . . an undefined zone between the inside and the outside," and the paratext "is made up of a heterogeneous group of practices and discourse of all kinds and dating from all periods" (Genette, 1–2). The eruption of these in the text rends and renders the real *body* of the transformed traces as fluid, fragmentary, technological. In advance of the internet but after the telegraph and film, Benjamin observed the spectacular and fragmentary qualities of modernity and interposed them into his own historical project. In the early nineteenth century, the Romantics saw ruins as a vital component in a fragmentary history that they could reconstitute. By the twentieth century, only the assemblage of fragments in juxtaposition remained. For Benjamin, the fragment established itself as the trope of the modern. Histories would need to be written not only for their times but to embody the forms of their times if awakening (the goal of history) was to be achieved. *The Arcades Project* embodied this trope of the modern in its very form. "To write history is to cite it" became the guiding principle of Benjamin's method in the Paris book. In his later *Theory of Film*, Siegfried Kracauer evokes a series of images from the movies of Fellini, De Sica, and Rossellini, and suggests not so much that they defy interpretation as that we should refuse the interpretative temptation the images seem so poignantly to present:

> Any attempt at an allegorical interpretation would drain these ideograms of their substance. They are propositions rather than rebuses. Snatched from transient life, they not only challenge the spectator to penetrate their secret but, perhaps even more insistently, request him to preserve them as the irreplaceable

images they are. (Wood, 15)

Castro's own experiences in dealing with issues like narrative and memory made him suspicious of the relationship between autobiography and truth. This doesn't mean that he believes that autobiography is inevitably a form of fiction, but that any form of writing, once produced, is subject to constant translation, and Castro extends the debate of fictional narrative and factual narration of an autobiographical writing to the inclusion of such paratextual forms as photographs, with a view to destabilizing any form of representation. In *Camera Lucida*, Roland Barthes (who features in *Birds of Passage*) offers another way of looking at photography and history, one that might seem to explain even better the paratextual attraction to photos within postmodern fiction. Photographs are said to carry their referent within themselves: there is a necessarily real thing which was once placed before the lens and which, while happening only once, can be repeated on paper.

Castro begins the fiction by quoting Franz Kafka's saying, "We photograph things in order to drive them out of our minds." This is supposedly a dialogue between Kafka and Gustav Janouch, as recorded in Barthes' *Camera Lucida*, and the words after that are "My stories are a way of shutting my eyes" (Barthes 1981, 53). In a paradoxical way, Kafka ransforms the photograph, a vehicle of remembrance, into something that expels a thing, a person, a place, a nightmare, out of the mind. In Kafka's formulation, the stories are a means of shutting our eyes, of not looking at things we are not willing to see. In this paradox, the relationship between photographs and fictions remains ambiguous. "On the one hand, stories are seen in contradistinction to photography—not as a means of exorcising demons, but rather as a means of shutting them out, of erecting a textual barrier between self and world. On the other hand, it is the relatedness of story to photograph that is intriguing, the sense in which writing too, may be an exorcism. 'Shutting the eyes,' as an act entailed in writing, would render narrative an effort both to expel and shut out the images that photography fixes" (Peucker, 663). In fictional autobiography, like *Shanghai Dancing*, it requires the use of memory, yet memory is quite fragmentary, incomplete, and inaccurate, so the postmodern fiction writers often resort to photography. In *Shanghai Dancing*, the narrator returned to Shanghai, trying to find out the traces of his life and his family life. He carries the photos left by his father, but even those photos do not work, as he feels not sure whether he can identify what is what. When he is in a situation of disorientation, he comes across Wu Kai-Ming, or Carmen Woo, who he later found is a professional photographer, but to his wonder, she said "she is not interested in recording the truth, but in *breaking the rules of reality*" (Castro 2003, 13). In a sense, what she states meets the requirements of postmodern sense of representation, in which photographs do not merely reproduce a pre-existing world, but constitute a highly coded discourse. Her interest in something other than reality makes the narrator aware of the doubleness of himself, as both narrator and narrated. The split between image of self and the self imaged, between the family and self, between self and the world. It is hard to imagine a text that would address the issue of representation as subversion more directly than this postmodern "autobiography"—which is also that of a mnemonic and tele-linguist hub, the text as migratory agent that internalizes and perpetuates a certain "translation" effect, actively negating, at every turn.

Traditionally the photograph is taken in the West as re-representation of nature, an unmediated transcription of reality onto film, something is "indexed" (in which the pointing finger or digit is evoked, as if a mute directing of the point, ignoring the finger, the figure of touch, digitalism, and so on). In this sense, it accords with the mimetic view, or ideology, of "translation" which Benjamin discretely retires. In terms of the image itself, a decisive word favored by Benjamin (the German *Bild*), something correspondingly goes on. "Image" is not, for him, about visual representation but a graphematic complex of memory traces, suffused by writing machines and archival force: like Chinese character writing it exceeds letteration, while hosting it. The photograph, as a form of writing, is for him an active mnemo-technic—and thus any intervention in "history" occurs, as with his project of "materialistic historio*graphy*" (*not* historical materialism), by altering the inscriptions, memory programming, archival settings, out of which futures are generated (or, as currently, it seems, pre-empted). Thus for Benjamin the photograph is a scene of reading, in which "light" itself is not originary but a technic of graphics and, as Eduardo Cadava has italicized, the photographic image is to be encountered as a tissue of *citations*. Benjamin remains relatively unique in collapsing this faux binary of Western aesthetics—which maintains a division between writing (and literature) and visual aesthetics (painting, film, and so on), a division with an unfortunate policing role in Western academic traditions (that is, descending from Plato's academy).

This ideological notion of *photography* as truthful documents endows the photography with the capacity to prove, to either present factual evidence or stand as a fact itself. It extends beyond Roland Barthes' assertion in *Camera Lucida* that "in Photography I can never deny that *the thing has been there*" (76), which marks ghostly mourning of anteriority at least, to an unquestioned acceptance that the photograph presents us with a faithful reproduction of what 'has been there.' The photography is a technological medium of transcription, light-writing (photographesis); it requires, Benjamin requires, active reading (when it is not merely consumed in and by a commodified image stream). It ruptures temporalities, mourning, ideologies of presence: it parallels the "dialectical image," which is precisely not *dialectical*. It is interpretative, rather than a piece of factual evidence, which positions the photograph too in or as a scene of *translation*. What the photographer communicates, if it can be called that, arises only from the figures we translate. Rather than presenting an evidential and singular truth, the photograph's silence invites the speculation of multiple citations, allowing it to be characterized as a "polylogue" (Sontag 2005, 136). (Cinema, which for Benjamin joins the chain leading from translation to "materialistic historiography," renders this citational frenzy hyperbolic.) It is this multiple haunting of the photograph, and its imbrication in a pictographic logic, that attracts Brian Castro to its eruption of a plurality of signs, speculations, and fantasies. As an alternative medium that draws attention to itself, and its technological premises, it "cites" the prehistories of its medium (and its futures) while marking writing, too, as such a medium by off-setting it. In one respect, it also stands in for what is absent in Shanghai Dancing but everywhere implied: Chinese writing, pictographics.

In the debate of the future of the novel in Australia, Castro shows his stance against the pragmatic, anti-intellectual ordinariness of the Australian mentality, embracing a challenge of "polyphony, or what I shall call *polyphony*. I would like to call this an art of the fugue, this assemblage of counterpoints and harmonious hybridities, this orchestration of fragmentary voices, polyphonia rather than polyphony. Not only multiple, but counterfeit. Not only multicultural, but linguistically invented. Not only polymorphous, but phon(e)y. We are threatened not by difference, but by sameness. Hybridity contains us. We are troubled when the monophonic leads us only to the forlornness of our entrenched identity" (Castro 2008, 127). What does "linguistically invented" point to, and why does Castro, in this nexus, caught up in the funhouse arcade of the Paris of the East, turn from the easy discourse of otherness, multiple identities, post-colonial debt and scarring, "multicultural" euphoria—as if a non-human technics asserts itself? Yet the literary "city" that echoes as a subtext of sorts may not be the Paris chosen as historical palimpsest of the *Arcades Project*, Castro comments, but Joyce's labyrinthine Dublin—only an unknown (to Castro) city referenced to his father's memories of it.[2] This refolding archeology requires a convolution of modernisms, self feeding ("I made it post-modern high modernism, and in a way flippant and playful"), and if anything Castro's "Shanghai" need be read not through the precision of *Ulysses*' Dublin but the disarticulations of tongues from the perspective of Benjamin's "pure language" of *Finnegan's Wake*—only the desideratum of the *ear* (for Joyce) is wanly displaced by that of the eye, in particular as regards the largely absent writing system that subtends and is "Shanghai," which compels the logics of the image, graphics, markings, the unreadable inscriptions, to play another ghost role in this pre-post-anti-inverse-high-modernist, which is to say perhaps a modernist writing—in so far as the 21st century, the era of post-global climate change in which localities are ghosted by the "non-human" and Shanghai is the poster child for the erasure of the past and the projection of the anonymous tele-megalopolis, stands outside the traces of both nostalgia and messianism that the perpetual unfolding of modernisms implied.

In the narration of the family history, Castro inserts many photographs. It seems that he is going to prove the truth of the narration, but the photos generate polyglot and polyphon(e)y interpretation. In one example, when he mentions that her his mother used to model for Levers in Shanghai, a photo of a beautiful young lady posing as a model for the Lever Brothers is presented, with the English title LEVER BROS CHINA LTD above and 利華公司出品 * 質料純淨 利華日光肥皂 * 去污迅速 on both sides. The photo asks to be read—even as it delves into the advertising world and fashion, disappeared and restored in unimaginably hyperbolic dimensions "today." Is it really a photo of her mother, or just a sample of a model? In the early days of Shanghai there are many advertising like this, and it is not difficult to find them. Is it used to mark the mixing of cultures as here both Chinese and English are provided without translation of either, or is it simply nostalgic of foreigners' interest in the East, like the American Ezra Pound, who appropriates Chinese texts too simply as ideograms and either translates them into English or simply displays its unreadability, like a violence within and to alphabeticism, as in his *Cantos*? Alphabeticism as a marking system of linear writing we associate, today, with the era of monotheism (and, in the West, that of "the Book")—that is, the specular interface of theology and "historical materialism" in its 20th century form, the twin pillars of catastrophic history, that the critic suspends at the opening of his *Theses on the Philosophy of History*. Is the "mother"— icon of genealogical purity, origin, nature itself in the West—a fake, necessarily? Is "she," perhaps not she, bedecked in a consumer fantasy to become blindingly totalized later, a doom? Does the *model* (and the term is double sided, as template or automaton), find herself positioned between the two languages, with Chinese appearing as the framing marking system, unreadable with the global Anglo imaginary the reader persists within? Does "she" represent the photographic image, its technicity and pre-linguistic writing, promote the contradictions of the Benjaminian "snapshot" (as explosive "dialectical image"), mechanical reproduction as the female form, hence a contradictory ur-writing, or "greater language" which has nothing to do with meaning as such but a catastrophic history underway? Can one stop or limit the proliferation of citations, here, or their artifice, which solicits and blocks mourning? Is it nothing but cited codes—in which repeat citations are reduced to superficial formalities?

V.

In a paper, "On Linguistic Aspects of Translation," Roman Jakobson identifies three categories of translation: intra-lingual, inter-lingual, and inter-semiotic, which is an interpretation of verbal signs by means of some other language (Jakobson, 114). This *semiotic* perspective on translation and interpretation, which hypostasizes languages as a code, is compelled to recognize the non-verbal aspects of language, especially images. This tradition of semiotics which at once codifies and deports content into an un-codified domain mimes a traditional divide between word and image—which Benjamin precisely called into question, and which something like the pictographic writing of China (or for Benjamin, differently, the photographic image) stand in for. According to this critical idiom, code-switching is classified as intra-sentential and inter-sentential, wherein switching occurs between sentences

(Bhatia and Ritchie, 283). Repeatedly the reader negotiates the inter-sentential use of the code-switching, as in: "Shanghai fremissait d'un bombardement loitain. M. Pomeroie était en train d'admirer le coucher du soleil, quand tout d'un coup, il se rendit compte que les couleurs merveilleux émanaient de son verger, qui etait en feu . . . " (Castro 2003, 145); or: "He wants to confer, to get it out into the open, or as the Chinese say, *seung leuhng*, to be virtuous together" (Castro, 344). Does this convey a poly-lingual and multicultural way of looking at (or for) *identities*, or does it mime that reflexive quest of today's reader as a commodified position?

The italicized text 商量 is supposed to be Chinese, but it is not in *pingyin* or the Wade-Giles system. Rather, it is a Cantonese way which shows the complexity even of his Chinese origin—and continues to cite "China" as the mysterious, unreadable background to a numb Orientalism (this time within "China"). The perpetual italicization of a lost translation recalls the purpose of the translator to create a hybrid identity. The intra-sentential code-switching includes *Nada a declarar* (171), *Bem-vindo papai* (157) *anxietas tibibarum* (152), *Esplendido* (150), *Mestizhina* (100); *pase cantes* (118), *paso doble* (119); *wallah-wallahs* frequently appear. Each can lead the reader into different linguistic worlds, but also—like the global dictionary entries for "whale" opening Melville's *Moby-Dick*—reduce these to recurrent syllables, letters, marked intervals. In each case, a haunting logic associated with colonialism is clear, and appears both inescapable and in some process of transformation, or passage. In one case the author displays a map of *Old Shanghai*, where street names are given in the colonial Latin names without any Chinese elements (267). These street names are widely seen in the author's Shanghai narratives. If we group them together we will find that the virtual map, as a paratext, tracks the colonial inscription through the present's presumed subversion of the same "colonialism"—at times converted into chic.

Latin Name	Colonial Translation	Modern Chinese name
Route Lafayette	辣斐德路	复兴中路
Rue Massenet	马斯南路	思南路
Seymour Road	西摩路	陕西北路
Baikal Road	倍开尔路	惠民路
Dixwell Road	狄思威路	溧阳路
Avenue Eduard VII	爱多亚路	延安东路
Rue Auguste Boppe	蒲柏路	太仓路
Rue Wantz	望志路	兴业路
Avenue du Roi Albert	亚尔培路	陕西南路
Avenue Dubail	吕班路	重庆南路
Route Ghisi	祁齐路	岳阳路
Route des Soeurs	圣母院路	瑞金一路
Route Vallon	环龙路	南昌路
Avenue Haig	海格路	华山路
Carter Road	卡德路	石门一路
Route J.Winling	汶林路	宛平路
Rubicon Road	罗别根路	哈密路
Avenue Joffre	霞飞路	淮海中路
Broadway	百老汇大厦	上海大厦
Richards Hotel	礼查饭店	上海浦江饭店

This diversion between place-names, as Proust would call them, is related to what Benjamin calls "image" without meaning anything overtly visual—so much as a mnemonic tangle out of which perception and the present arise perpetually. Here, in "Shanghai," one might say, as with these place-names, the second pictographic script is at once ghosted by the "colonial" super-imposition, prehistorial to it (as image is to letter), and an allegorical stand in for the logics of "pure language" going back to our opening remarks—of which Chinese, unreadable script, is the place-holder. If the *Passagenwerke* required and took Paris as their palimpsest, Shanghai as the "Paris of the East" incorporates not the petrie dish of Euro-modernity but that of the 21st century, post-global tele-mediatric world rebalancing to Asia.

What sets "Shanghai" dancing, then, if that name, and its inscriptions, names the text and the histories of transport and translation that present a historical horizon that cannot belong definitively to any identify or even language, any family memory—since the era of climate change, we might say, is neither modernist nor post-modernist, but that before which a species question is posed, not that of a national history. Thus, something about Shanghai, presented as two characters (上海), is set *dancing* too within this temporal city-scape, within graphics, without meaning or content. Of course, 上海 means "above the sea," dating from the 11th century Song Dynasty, and the two would be reversible in order: "above the sea," "the sea . . . above," or literally "on" or "against" the sea—assuming we know what a "sea" is, in its verbal labyrinths, its surfaces and liquid support of "life" and visibility, a semiosis worked by writers like Conrad and Melville. Other older names include *Shen* (the name of an ancient noble and hero), and *Huating* (the first administrating of the modern city initiated in Songjiang—where this essay is being composed at this moment of writing).

What we saw at the beginning was a dissonance within the concept of translation that harassed Benjamin's text and posed questions related to the post-global horizons emerging today, particularly in the context of the fold between Chinese pictographic writing and Western alphabeticism and the residue of "global" English. Just when one thought, in Benjamin, that translation opens onto the experience of the cultural "other," as we say, we noted it turned elsewhere entirely, was unconcerned with identity and otherness, marked instead the "non-human" with respect to language itself, putting in question the "human" as a cognitive or species question. To shift from Paris, Capital of the 19th Century, to Shanghai, the Paris of the East, Capital of . . . is to shift, in any case, outside of an Anglo-centric history. While the need to posit "cultural" difference and "post-colonial" formations of justice saturates and orients our experience of history, it distracts us from the ominous extra-anthropic factors that impinge on and intervene in 21st century prospects. This last "shift" or translation, from cultural differences and the human politics of historical victimage and memory to an era of "climate change" that puts the multiplicity of tongues (and memory technologies) into a species perspective collectively presents another dimension of translation itself arguably—and introduces a hyperbolic and auto-differing reading scene, an agenealogical dance of extinctions, ghosts, wounds, against which one active resistance, and shuttle, involves *not* identifying with "identities."

    Thus an inherent logic of Benjaminian *translation* goes hyper, and undergoes another translation (of) itself. Anthony Appiah, in discussing the marginalized other, proposes a concept of *thick translation* to mine the depths of ethnic cultures, and so as to give the marginalized and long silenced *other* an opportunity to be represented. By *thick translation* is meant a way to seek, "with its annotations and its accompanying glosses to locate the text in a rich cultural and linguistic context. . . . A thick translation of the context of literary production, a translation that draws on and creates that sort of understanding, meets the need to challenge ourselves and our students to go further, to undertake the harder project of a genuinely informed respect for others" (Venuti, 427). And yet, this ignores where translation, like what Benjamin calls allegory, "negates" what it names as a "present's" memory programming. It is the logic of translation *itself* which, as in the German writer, turns from and empties out the crafted forms of cultural difference and the artifice of subjectivities (as "others") that critical culture has fed upon—even as its academic clout and import degenerated in the first decade of this supposedly new "millennium," and as "politics" appears emptied out, certainly in the West and the post-democratic mediacracies and neo-feudal financialization whose exponential drives seem, for the moment, to carve out a new set of horizons that do not gel with modernisms or post-modernisms. Brian Castro's "Shanghai" as a non-site is situated in this linguistico-transitional event, like a train station or Grand Central Station of these mutually enfolded and imposed agenealogies that subsist in the historical backglance that posits a faux auto-biography of an "East" and a "West." If Brian Castro's performance recalls the ending of Yeats "Among School Children"—that is, if it asks, "How can we know the dancer from the dance?"—it is not in the sense of an auto-biographical truth (the dancer) nor a dance that cannot repeat itself in the same way or escape the need to do so. Castro's writing machine dances over and on the feet of effaced inscriptions of the pictographic subtext, generating the hybridities it subverts as non-identities. It does so seemingly by way of a pre-historical trace that gestures toward a (non)maternal runic writing (Chinese? Photography's) which does not arrive with a cipher and foregrounds a post-global afterlife which is not that of "other subjectivities" whose shared "experience" would be recovered as some cherished or mourned "vessel." It is something that brings the *non-human* as global and terrestrial process together with the non-human of inscriptive practices, and the latter's technological accelerations—it is translation as hyperbolic process rather than translation as the fetishization of proper meaning, outside the Western laws of mimesis that, in fact, powered the latter's ravenous trajectories. This positions *Shanghai Dancing*, potentially, at this 21st century crease in writing systems that is agenealogical, finally, and to which one gives the name *Shanghai*.

Notes:

1 See also Stuart Beaton, "A journey from a Macao ferry to kangaroos and back." http://www.chinadaily.com.cn/life/2011–04/29/content_12419138.html and Marilyne Brun. "'Grammars of Creation': An interview with Brian Castro." 24 November 2008. *The Journal of the European Association of Studies on Australia*, Vol.2. No.1, 2011, www.ub.edu/dpfilsa/jeasa24castro.pdf

2 Cited in Beaton: "I made Dublin into Shanghai. Joyce was unique in that he was in Trieste, and he never went back to Dublin to look up these streets or get the atmosphere, he just asked friends, 'What's that pub there?' or 'Was it like that?' just to get the accuracy. I did the same with my father's Shanghai, I could never get inside his mind or discover the Shanghai of the 30s. I was lost—but in order to get the flavor of that time, I needed to return to the canon, and the canon was high modernism. So I made it post-modern high modernism, and in a way flippant and playful."

References:

Barker, Karen. "Theory as Fireworks: An Interview with Brian Castro," *Australian Literary Studies*, 20.3 (2002). Print.

Barthes, Roland. *Camera Lucida: Reflections on Photography*. Trans. Richard Howard. New York: Hill and Wang, 1981. Print.

Bassnett, Susan, and André Lefevere. *Constructing Cultures: Essays on Literary Translation*. Multilingual Matters, 1998. Print.

Beaton, Stuart. "A journey from a Macao ferry to kangaroos and back." <http://www.chinadaily.com.cn/life/2011–04/29/content_12419138.html>.

Benjamin, Walter. "The Task of the Translator," *Illuminations*. Trans. Harry Zohn. New York: Schocken Books, 2007. Print.

Bermann, Sandra, and Michael Wood, eds. *Nation, Language, and the Ethics of Translation*. New Jersey: Princeton University Press, 2005. Print.

Bhatia, Tej K. and William C. Ritchie. *The Handbook of Bilingualism*. Oxford: Blackwell Publishing, 2004. Print.

Brennan, Bernadette. *Brian Castro's Fiction: The Seductive Play of Language*. Amherst, New York: Cambria Press, 2008. Print.

Brun, Marilyne. "'Grammars of Creation': An interview with Brian Castro." *The Journal of the European Association of Studies on Australia*. 2, 1, 2011 <www.ub.edu/dpfilsa/jeasa24castro.pdf>.

Buse, Peter. *Benjamin's Arcades: An Unguided Tour*. Manchester University Press, 2006. Print.

Castro, Brian. *Looking for Estrellita*. St. Lucia: University of Queensland Press, 1999. Print.

——. *Shanghai Dancing*. Giramondo, 2003. Print.

——. "Making Oneself Foreign." *Meanjin*. 64.4 (Dec. 2005). Print.

——. "Arrested Motion and Future-Mourning: Hybridity and Creativity." *Southerly*, 68.3 (Autumn 2008). Print.

Cronin, Michael. *Translation and Identity*. London & New York: Routledge, 2006. Print.

De Man, Paul. "Autobiography as De-facement." *MLN*, Vol. 94, No. 5 (Dec. 1979). Print.

Frisby, David. *Fragments of Modernity: Theories of Modernity in the Work of Simmel, Kracauer, and Benjamin*. Cambridge: MIT Press, 1988. Print.

Genette, Gerard. Paratexts: *Thresholds of Interpretation*. Cambridge: Cambridge University Press, 1997. Print.

Jakobson, Roman. "On Linguistic Aspects of Translation." *The Translation Studies Reader*. Ed. Lawrence Venuti. London and New York: Routledge, 2000. Print.

Ommundsen, Wenche. "Multiculturalism, Identity, Displacement." *From a Distance: Australian Writers and Cultural Displacement*. Eds. Wenche Ommundsen and Hazel Rowley. Geelong: Deakin University Press, 1996. Print.

Peucker, Brigitte. "Kubrick and Kafka: The Corporeal Uncanny." *Modernism/Modernity* 8.4 (2001). Print.

Sontag, Susan. *On Photography*. Rosetta Books, LLC, 2005. Print.

Venuti, Lawrence, ed. *The Translation Studies Reader*. London & New York: Routledge, 2000. Print.

Wood, Michael. "Fragments of Modernity." *A Century of Books*. New Jersey, Princeton: Princeton University Press, 2005. Print.

Facing the Global by Way of the Multicultural:
A Look into Antipodean Women Storytellers

Shiao-Ying SHEN

National Taiwan University, Taiwan

> I live in a room and it isn't home. I live in Australia—and it isn't home. I live on earth—and it isn't home. With everyone I meet I feel alien. Except you. You're weird, but you seem familiar. I catch myself imagining you're from the real world. The one I dream about. The one I'd pray existed.
>
> Wayne, *The Rivers of China* (I viii)
> (De Groen, 29)

How do women storytellers face, process and respond to the complexities of globalization? This paper presents the work of six women artists as a way of considering this question. Among these six, two are dramatists, one a visual artist, and three filmmakers. These storytellers are a multicultural group, and they draw from their varied cultures when pondering the challenges of globalization. New Zealander Alma De Groen and Melburnian Hannie Rayson tap into their cultural roots and explore gender, social and political issues in plays such as *The Rivers of China* and *Inheritance*. Visual artist Tracey Moffatt employs her Aboriginal connection in her photo series and short films when negotiating the global art scene. Filmmakers Jane Campion and Sue Brooks engage sexual and local images in their feature films to navigate the many challenges in the world of commercial narrative film. Clara Law, a filmmaker who migrated from Hong Kong, writes a filmic "letter to Oz" with her *Letters to Ali*, and assuages her decades-long anxiety of culture, locating a sense of home through her documentation of diasporic cultures. In the following collage of the works of these storytellers, this paper offers a picture of the ways in which women artists from Down Under tackle the forces of globalization.

Dramatists Down Under

Around the turn of the millennium, both Alma De Groen and Hannie Rayson produced plays which consider the state of women's social evolution after half a century of conscious strivings. Both *Wicked Sisters* (2002) and *Life After George* (2000) plant a dead male in the center of their plot. Both plays concentrate on their female characters' response to the death of the male, facilitating a review of the choices made by these females during a period of history when choices—intellectual, sexual, economic—were allowed to women. De Groen and Rayson's concern for women's situation and gender positions are clear and compelling; however, the place where these playwrights excel is in their dramatic configuration of their response to globalization, in their highlighting of their characters' struggle with multicultural entanglements. Both *Wicked Sisters* and *Life After George* target the corporatization of intellectual institutions—globalization in academia—and offer up four women's stories as critical ways of addressing the issue.

With *Wicked Sisters*, Alma De Groen shaped and dramatized the dead male in the form of a ghostly computer which still emits sounds and formulations even after the demise of its master. This design in *Wicked Sisters* showcases De Groen's skill at locating junctions where science and technology interact with globalized existence.[1] Furthermore, for DeGroen, the female perspective, sometimes with the aid of persuaded male efforts, is often the stance with which authoritarian and totalizing global forces are countered. Hannie Rayson, on the other hand, with her Melburnian *Life After George*,[2] is adept at formulating familial sagas, weaving a web of intricate human relations to sift out the evolution of globalization that is often behind the fortunes of her plays' charismatic males.

Although, with *Wicked Sisters* and *Life After George*, Alma De Groen and Hannie Rayson have both located similar vibes of globalization in the form of corporatization of intellectual institutions, each playwright has produced other works which further effectively highlight how antipodean culture interacts with controlling global forces. De Groen's *The Rivers of China* (1987) and *The Woman in the Window* (1998) and Rayson's *Inheritance* (2003) are such works. With these plays, De Groen and Rayson show that globalization can manifest itself through the all-encompassing force of the North, through the English tales and plots from the northern hemisphere that can obliterate the narratives from the South. The way in which De Groen and Rayson counter these northern forces is by turning to their roots and their land, recounting tales related to the Down Under.

Alma De Groen, an antipodean dramatist born in New Zealand, addresses the crushing force of the North by way of asserting her cultural roots in *The Rivers of China*, a play which studies the final days of New Zealand's storyteller Katherine Mansfield. Alma De Groen, in the 1970s, after four years of working in the North, returned to Australia (where she moved to in 1964) and produced short and full-length plays. In 1987, with *The Rivers of China*, De Groen dramatized Katherine Mansfield's ultimate attempt at moving away from the mainstream to experiment with the alternative. By giving primacy to Mansfield's final year, to her stay at George Gurdjieff's school at Fontainebleau, *The Rivers of China* presents Mansfield traveling away from her English husband to attempt a last exploration—a recuperation of her mind and body at a compound for alternative healing. De Groen then temporally juxtaposes Mansfield's days at Fontainebleau in 1922 with "a present" set in a Sydney hospital. Aside from this temporal and geographic design, this crisscrossing between 1922 Fontainebleau and present-day Sydney, the gender structure of *The Rivers of China* also embodies a resonant juxtaposition: Mansfield's discriminated experience at Gurdjieff's compound is paired with a Sydney man's disoriented struggle in a futuristic present where gender power relations have been reversed. In the present Sydney, instead of early 20th century repression of women, we are shown a place where "there are no books by men" (De Groen II iv, 45).

By designing such a temporal and gender structure, De Groen proffers a metaphorical concept of form,[3] through which she opens up a space where gender relations intertwines with cultural history and matters of art, where the paralleling of two time-frames sheds light on the power relations of different cultures. The effect of De Groen's dramatic form shows itself in the play's explication of the problem it wishes to debate and in the formulation of an antidote to the malaise which engulfs her characters. In a time when globalization seemingly provides constant digitized interconnectedness, Alma De Groen's work stresses our paradoxical sense of alienation. In her tales, characters cannot feel a sense of home except in cultural presences which relate to one's own roots. In the case of *The Rivers of China*, the presence is "a you that seems familiar"; for the repressed and "homesick" male in the play, the presence is Katherine Mansfield. Alma De Groen employs Katherine Mansfield to inject not only a Down Under sensibility into *The Rivers of China*, but also a desire and a bold imagining of how gender equity and "root culture" could alleviate "the homesickness" that ails Sydney-siders in the age of globalization.

A decade after *The Rivers of China*, the dramatic structuring of diverse time and space is again employed by Alma De Groen in *The Woman in the Window* (1998). This play foregrounds even further women's history and experience. Another female artist, the Russian modernist poet Anna Akhmatova, is employed and set in the repressive Stalinist Leningrad of the 1950s; and a "confidence girl" in the service work force, Rachel Sekerov, is set in "Australia, a future." The Australia in *The Woman in the Window* is a place where the digital and the virtual takes over, where a poet is a person who does not write poetry but someone who can access digital archives to monopolize an item (such as "the moon") in past poems for study; this item then becomes the poet's "market niche" in the futuristic super-society. This juxtaposition, this setting up of North (Soviet Russia) and South (future Australia), makes possible an imagined evasion of past and future repressive states, an evasion which pressures us to work out a liberal present, and pushes for a reaching across time, for a fusing of the power of words and imagination to the force of technology and science in hope for a more enlightened existence. De Groen's time-space dialectics produces an imagined "present," an enlightened existence, a possible "home" for those who suffer and question: "For a long time I stood at the gate of

Hell/ But Hell was closed/ Even the Devil didn't need me./ So where should I go?" (I xiv)[4] De Groen's dramaturgy suggests that the power of great art can subvert the coercive forces that exercise control in societies, and can provide us with "the yellow line" directing us in our desire to find home and to "go home."[5]

Alma De Groen uses cultures of different times, whether they are of the North or of the South, as another form of multiculturalism to counter the oppressive force of political regimes or the economic rationalism and industrial mega-corporations of our futuristic-present. De Groen's countering stance against globalization is not only embodied in the multiplicity of culture,[6] but also anchored to female sensibility, creativity and solidarity. *The Woman in the Window* presents "future Australia" as a dystopian super-society where women's writings have been eradicated from the digital literary archive, buried into the deep archives; it is through female connection across time, through the "supernatural" meeting of Akhmatova and Rachel, together with the guidance of a female muse, that a possible freeing of female writing, a more nourishing existence can emerge.

While Alma De Groen skillfully parallels past political surveillance with future technological surveillance; Hannie Rayson, on the other hand, does not engage in the distant or the futuristic; her plays firmly stems from the Australian present. Rayson often focuses on a troubling social phenomenon of her time, probes its causes, tracks its evolution, and hammers out a dramatic structure through which the problem can be approached and deliberated.

In *Inheritance* (2003) Hannie Rayson targets the conservative political force and its social and economic practices that enveloped much of Australia at the turn of the millennium.[7] The play tells a story of the land, of its inheritance and dispossession. *Inheritance* does not bring in actual political figures, nor does it counter the conservative force by way of a gender position as De Groen does; the play reflects on its issue by way of setting up a multitude of careworn Australian lives strongly connected to the land; and through these lives, the play brings forth the ineptness and hollowness of a long line of land-related political practices and tenets. *Inheritance* focuses on the 80th birthday of a pair of twin sisters, tells the story of four generations of Australian rural life, and presents to us the points at which "dominant ideas meet lived experience."[8] Rayson, by way of a family saga, through the tensions between the families of the twin sisters, brings together the urban and the country, the heterosexual and the homosexual, mainstream and aboriginal culture, the past and the present. The family in *Inheritance* is very much a microcosm of Australia, and Rayson's weaving together of this family tapestry draws out the colonialism, the racism, the economic evolution that is tangled within this tricky family terrain, this Australian history.

What Alma De Groen achieves in *The Rivers of China* and *The Woman in the Window* is to convey the desire and delineate the possibility of evading the tyranny of gendered power and the violence of oppressive regimes. Hannie Rayson reveals in *Inheritance* the complex realities of rural life, brings heightened clarity to the situation in rural Australia, highlights the spreading impact of globalization, and in the end enables a more enlightened critical stance to the complicated situation.

Visual Artist Tracey Moffatt[9]

In the area of visual arts, Tracey Moffatt's work demonstrates a different maneuvering of the global-multicultural dynamics. It is the aesthetic, the style, the look of Moffatt's work that first attracts attention, and the style which she employs is the "globally-friendly" kind. The look of her work, often using sumptuous and stunning colors, has been identified as embodying "glossiness" and "glamour." Also, Moffatt does not shy away from using alluring or voluptuous female bodies to hold our gaze. Moffatt exploits this style, which possesses global currency, to represent local stories. In other words, Moffatt appropriates a global style to empower her unveiling of entrancing Australian stories.

Tracey Moffatt is an artist whose work has been showcased in New York City's Dia Center in 1997, and whose films and videos have been distributed by Ronin Films in DVD form.[10] What is seductive in Moffatt's work is that, even in her individual photographs, one can sense the call of an entrancing story: her work invites you to approach it, to gaze at it, luring you with the promise of a secret about to be unveiled.[11] The female body in her work is not de-sexed but milked for all it can suggest. In her 1989 *Something More* still photograph series, one picture (#3) has the very *guapa*[12] Moffatt herself in a bright red-and-black floral patterned high-slit *qipao* (cheongsam, Chinese high-collared close fitting dress) sitting in an ocher setting with a pigtailed young Asian man dreamily laying his head on her lap. This 98 x 127 cm photo seems to invite one to project onto it the "melodrama of land, settlement and violence" (Martin, 13–15), to think back on and imagine the pioneering golden days, the mixing of white, Chinese, Aboriginal presences, and its synchronous or subsequent violence of assimilation and eradication.

In her work, Moffatt gives us sumptuous colors or haunting black and white (as in her *Laudanum* series, 1998); she invites us to gaze, and in that gazing allow the pain and uncanniness of history to emerge, displacing our expectant moment of melodramatic indulgence.

If a Moffatt photo teases us with such associative dramas, then her films evoke intense sensual thinking.[13] Moffatt's 1990 *Night Cries—A Rural Tragedy* (17 minutes),[14] with its stunning color, smooth and jarring aural treatment, hits one with the wounds and tenderness of an Australian maternal melodrama. This short film opens and ends with Jimmy Little's performance of his 1964 hit "Royal Telephone." The Aboriginal showman's velvety singing draws one into an outback mother-daughter story. Moffatt's short film, shot on a soundstage, conveys a daughter's sense of entrapment caring for a withering mother while recalling tender and loving childhood moments; and the soundtrack's railroad sounds amplifies the daughter's desire to flee from the heat and dryness of outback life. As we are shown the daughter (played by the fleshy Marcia Langton) hosing and cooling herself down with water, the film's hot and stifling present is intercepted with snippets of childhood memory, with childhood's beachside play and comforting moments with the mother. In other words, the film simultaneously highlights the oppressiveness and the "warmth" of heat. All the film's compelling audio-visual elements—the daughter's dark voluptuous body and the pale mother's gnarled aged feet, Jimmy Little's crooning and the frustrating radio static, bare outback setting and dramatic studio colors—compose a luscious and tainted Australian melodrama, luring us into the harsh reality of assimilation, unsettling us with the tenderness present in that hard history.

Laleen Jayamanne, in her excellent analysis of *Night Cries*, has noted the "suspicious" glossiness of the film, but also sees in it "a certain unusual daring in Australian cinema." She shows how Moffatt performs a complex mediation which achieves in suggesting the possibility of reconciliation even before the idea became state policy.[15] Whether it is the "glossiness" or the "frank glamour" critics note in Moffatt (Martin 15), the sensuousness or the pleasure one experiences in her work, they do not undercut the overt political meaning of her texts. In this age of the "post" (post-capitalist, post-modern, post-colonial . . .), the pleasure Moffatt offers does not so much attempt to counter the objectifying gaze but rather draws out our awareness of the complicity of pleasure, the power of pleasure to lure one to see, feel, and learn.[16] Moffatt appropriates global aesthetics to lure us into a glimpse of the multiplicity of Australian culture.

Filmmaker Jane Campion

In the area of commercial narrative film, women filmmakers maneuver the global-multicultural dynamics in varied ways.

Jane Campion, perhaps the most globally-known Australian female director, is recognized as a filmmaker of woman-centered stories. What often identifies and undermines Campion's narratives is her intense focus on romance and the sexual side of female experience, and everything in her films serves that exploration. When asked about her choice of the Maori elements and landscape in *The Piano* (1993), a film which established Campion in the international scene, Campion admitted that she does not know Maori culture very well, and that the film "could have inserted more Maori elements but they wouldn't have been integrated into the story"; as to the New Zealand landscape, Campion thought the wild landscape suited the story because it could highlight the harshness and darkness in romanticism, manifesting nature as something "greater than you, your spirit or humanity even" (Caputo and Burton, 75). When speaking of *Holy Smoke*'s Australian outback, Campion emphasizes the "transcendent" sense of the vast landscape shots:

> There are marvelous, beautiful certainties that we can forget: the sun coming up, the moon, night and day. All these are very important to me. The inexorable movement of the earth, from day to night, night to day, gives certainty. No matter where you go, these things go on. (Murphy, 35)

Campion constantly desires to transcend the local and reach for the great beyond.[17]

It then comes as no surprise that critics would read the outback in Campion's *Holy Smoke* (1999) as belonging to a "mythic zone" (Murphy, 35) or embodying the "post-national"—"a spatiality in transit, a vulnerable geography of fleeing connection" (Polan, 155). Campion's urge to go beyond the local has also been perceived as a postmodern impulse in which nature and the body become vehicles to articulate a spiritual materialism, a desire for something that escapes and exceeds human meanings (Alemany-Galway, 320). Unlike Tracey Moffatt, whose staged ocher outback highlights the local and allows locality and all its historicity and political-ness to emerge, Campion's landscapes always point toward somewhere else: Campion's local does not want to stay local.

Campion's use of landscape can be wanting, how then does her staging of sexual politics, which all other elements in her films ultimately serve, perform? Many might agree that the most striking image in *Holy*

Smoke is that of Kate Winslet's naked body set against the outback terrain. With all its youthful potency and vulnerability, Winslet's body, while a powerful weapon in her sexual battle against the male deprogrammer (played by Harvey Keitel), does not have the sense of history the clothed and more aged body of Marcia Langton in *Night Cries* can communicate, nor does it have the sensuality, the sense of pressing and frustrated desire Langton's fleshiness can embody. Other Campion films show similar "diminished" female bodies. Ada's (Holly Hunter) body in *The Piano* is sedately framed like an oil painting's gothic nude, quietly declaring Ada's choice of the sensory world; and in Campion's *In the Cut* (2003), a film promising sexual explicitness from the outset, the slim Meg Ryan is paired with the wholesome and still a bit boyish Mark Ruffalo—a pairing which feels more like a casting for a romantic comedy.

In the Cut's sex scenes show a tameness that queries the strong attraction and *fear* the Meg Ryan character experiences in her sexual encounters with the "worldly, tough, a little over the hill . . . corrupt emotionally" macho Detective Malloy.[18] The coupling of Ryan and Ruffalo undermines the edginess and danger that we expect from a suspense thriller and from the dynamics between the leading couple. If, as Campion herself has stressed, *In the Cut* is about probing "the romantic myth in Western society,"[19] if it is a story in which "sex and the body are where the truth lies" (Francke, 19), then while we do see the body (even a close-up of an erect penis in the Australian release—a prosthesis was cast for it), there is, in the bodily encounters, moistness and humidity but not the heat needed to drive the film toward some form of revelation. Campion's sexual stagings are constantly just one image away from the starkly "sexual."

Campion sets *In the Cut* in post-9/11 New York, but places its harrowing climax scene in an abstracted, phallic lighthouse. *In the Cut*, a film whose truth is supposed to lie in sex and the body, in order to get an R-rating instead of an NC-17 rating in the American market, cuts out shots of an erect penis from the film's American version. *In the Cut*, like Campion's other works, refuses to totally bask in locality and sexuality.

Reconciliator Sue Brooks[20]

Campion's juggling of the sexual and the universal in her films is one instance of how an Australian female director navigates her way in the global film scene. Another such instance can be found in Sue Brooks' *Japanese Story* (2003), a film which engages a Japanese man to examine the intercultural zone within Australia.

Japanese Story names its Japanese man Hiromitsu Tachibana and its Australian female protagonist Sandy Edwards. Brooks' Hiromitsu is both an introspective tourist and a potential shopper/buyer, going on a road trip to the exotic Australian outback, interested in what the iron-red land could yield. Brooks' story sends the geologist Sandy (played by Toni Collette) and the businessman Hiro (Gotaro Tsunashima) on a trek to the deserts of the Pilbara region in Western Australia. What Brooks stresses in her Japanese man is his capital, his potential powerful capacity to purchase, to buy valued extractions from the land; still, Hiro, this foreigner, is very much employed to probe the psychic interiority of the Australian female. This Japanese man, the foreigner, exists to service the delineation of the Australian identity.

Japanese Story kills off its Japanese in an accident a little more than halfway into the film, and the rest of the film is immersed in the internal struggles of Sandy as she tries to comprehend this sudden loss. Brooks openly states that *Japanese Story* is "just her [Sandy] story, and from her point of view, it's as simple as that" (Cancela, 21). In order to tell Sandy's Australian story, the film needs the shock of an Other, a foreigner; it needs a subdued Japanese story. The Japanese story in Brooks' film involves a sensual, sexual connection between their leads. In their encounter, the Japanese male becomes the object of desire; we the audience and the film's female lead are the holder of the gaze. In other words, the Japanese male is feminized so as to bring out qualities in the Australian female. In *Japanese Story* Sandy gazes at Hiro's lean and soft-lined body as he finishes a swim; in the film's sex scene, Sandy puts on Hiro's pants and gets on top of him while he remains still and naked. Felicity Collins, in her "*Japanese Story*: A Shift of Heart," considers Toni Collette as playing "a quintessential Australian role, a role honed into national recognition through a series of iconic performances of Australian masculinity by the likes of Chips Rafferty, Bill Hunter, Bryan Brown, Jack Thompson and Ray Barrett" (Collins, 2003). If we consider a kind of "hard men," "mateship" as an essential part of Australian self-identity, then Toni Collette represents Australianness and conveys that masculine quality in female form; the Japanese man thus needs to be, and is conveniently, feminized to highlight Sandy's Aussieness. More simply put, the sexual, gender and cultural dynamics in *Japanese Story* prove to be highly interested in empowering Sandy, in stressing Sandy's experience, in telling an Australian story.

The sexual contact with the foreigner in *Japanese Story* serves as the triggering factor for the Australian Sandy to begin and accept a process of reflection and reconciliation. The connection with a foreigner in *Japanese Story* aids the very Australian and very female production team of Sue Brooks, Alison Tilson (writer), and Sue Maslin (producer) to bring out a new element in the Australian identity. While Hiro is feminized, Sandy is given a more masculine identity; this roughness, "undaintiness," in the image of the Australian female is not new in Australian cinema (e.g. the sheep tending Aussie female is contrasted with the elegant English wife in Michael Blakemore's 1994 *Country Life*); what is added in *Japanese Story* is the incorporation of a struggling and softening reflectiveness in the Aussie Sandy after her encounter with, and sudden loss of, the feminized Hiro.

In many narratives, foreign eyes, foreigners are employed to help underscore their story's themes, concerns, or the situation of their protagonists. Sue Brooks uses a Japanese man to obliquely touch upon an Australian issue. As one reads the articles on *Japanese Story*, one notices how the film is associated with works of desert journeys such as *Walkabout* (1971) and *The Goddess of 1967* (2000); but in the Australian writings, there are also observations of a political aspect in this intimate film. Lorena Cancela, in her preface to her interview with Sue Brooks, detects a political dimension in the film's mourning ritual. She sees Sandy's mourning of Hiro resonating with events in contemporary Australian society, events related to Australia's indigenous Aboriginal population (Cancela, 18). Felicity Collins states it more clearly. Collins detects a post-Mabo consciousness in *Japanese Story* (Mabo refers to the High Court case in 1993 that opened the way to selective restoration of native title to land in Australia). In Collins' reading of the film, she explicitly points out that "Sandy's inchoate struggle to meet her social obligations to show remorse and accept guilt resonates with the post-Mabo politics of reconciliation" (Collins 2004, 182). In other words,

Japanese Story elicits in white Australians a process of facing the loss, of accepting the regret, of reconciling with the entangled and traumatic engagement of white Australia with the Aborigines. While Cancela suggests that this process might be functioning "on an unconscious level" (Cancela, 18), *Japanese Story* actually makes conscious its social concerns in its insertion of the Yothu Yindi song "Treaty" at the beginning of the film by way of having the foreigner Hiromitsu play the track in his hired car.

Yothu Yindi is an Australian multiracial band; their 1991 single, "Treaty," won all sorts of awards.[21] The song signaled a high point when Aboriginal culture gained access to the popular imagination. At the same time, the events surrounding the song also marked the ironic rejection of Aboriginality by mainstream society: during the time of the band's honored recognition, the Aboriginal leader of the band was refused service in a St Kilda bar in Melbourne, allegedly on grounds of his color. "Treaty" sings of, "Words are easy, words are cheap/ Much cheaper than our priceless land. . . . This land was never given up/ This land was never bought and sold." By playing this song at the beginning of the film—at Hiromitsu's arrival in the Australian desert—*Japanese Story* is calling on its Australian viewers' collective unconscious and nudging them towards a certain way of experiencing the film.

This political element in *Japanese Story* underwent, like Campion's *In the Cut*, a "trimming" process. Commercial narrative film is the most globalized product amongst the visual arts, and films from Down Under always have to contend with the American market. What *Japanese Story* conceded when confronted with the American market was to cut away the film's opening—Hiromitsu's arrival in Australia and his playing of the Yothu Yindi track in his rented car. Ironically, Sue Brooks, in her commentary in the special features of the DVD, claims that the cut was to make it easier for the American viewers to see the film as Sandy's story. In other words, to make the film friendlier for US viewers, *Japanese Story* focuses more on Sandy, seemingly crafting it into more of an Australian story, but in fact taking away elements within the narrative that highlight Australian social and political reflections. To make the film global, it cuts down on the local.

Another instance of this concession occurs in the part where Sandy struggles with Hiro's dead body. In the American version of *Japanese Story*, the struggle was cut short. And much is lost. In the Australian version, the long duration of Sandy's sustained struggle with dead weight allows one not only to witness Sandy's desperation, but also experience a gamut of emotions as Sandy tries to move Hiro's body into the van. Sandy's initial shock, panic, and awkward attempts at dragging the body seem funny, then her earnestness becomes affecting, and finally her female physical effort with the dead weight comes to be heartrending. It is through following the duration of Sandy's exertion and despair that we come closer to Sandy, and it is through having experienced this weighty process with Sandy that we come to appreciate the sincerity in her later expression of remorse. Again, by cutting down the local to suit the global, *Japanese Story*'s American edition slims down to become a less resonant Australian story.

Migrant Clara Law

A "later-comer" to this antipodean global-multicultural contention is Clara Law, an already established filmmaker who emigrated from Hong

Kong during the territory's transition in the 1990s. After directing a couple of feature narrative films related to her new home Australia, in 2004 Clara Law released her documentary, *Letters to Ali*. Documentary has never been Law's preferred film form; she took on this form as a means to address the asylum debates which was forced onto the public scene by the policies of the Howard government. With the aid of digital cameras, Law was able to present her more intimate take on the issue. Law included herself in the narrative, recorded the trips of the Kerbi family, and tried to capture the confined state of Ali, the young Afghan asylum seeker. This recording encompassed at least three cultures, and the film's footage of the changing landscape of Australia from south to north shows the multiplicity of land. *Letters to Ali* can be seen as a documentary which highlights the multicultural to not only question political policies, but also to investigate the trans-national and border-crossing practices of today's globalization. Clara Law, through the medium of documentary, this less commercialized form, found a means with which she could more immediately reflect on the values of her adopted home.

Letters to Ali records the Kerbi family's 2003 road trip, a journey from the southern Melbourne part of Victoria to the north-western town of Port Hedland in Western Australia. The aim of the trip was to visit a young Afghan asylum seeker held at the Port Hedland detention center. The film, shot with digital cameras, reveals three aspects of the journey: the Kerbi family's desire to accommodate the Afghan teenager and extract him from the detention center; the sentiments of the young Afghan as expressed through his letters to Trish Kerbi; and Clara Law's own ruminations in the form of word texts about the road trip, about her own migration, about Australia.

"Ali" is the alias given to the Afghan boy in detention; to further protect his identity, the face of Ali is never clearly shown; one can say, Ali does not have much of a face or voice in the film. *Letters to Ali* is for the most part the Kerbi family's response to Ali's situation, but it is very much framed and colored under Law's own detached and melancholic visual tone. The film comes through like Law's own letters to Australia. Law's decision to voice her sentiments in the form of typed-on word texts corresponds to the epistolary format taken on by this documentary. Law abandons her past virtuosic stylistic displays, and allows the digital camera to record the trip, to capture the range of Australian light and terrain with least filter mediation. With this documentary, Law travels far within the island continent, and comes closer to formulating her own picture of Australia.

It has been a decade-long process through which Clara Law came to learn about how to visually represent her adopted home. The process started with the short *Wonton Soup* (1994), in which there was only a mentioning of Australia by its characters. With the three-continental *Floating Life* (1996), about half of the film presents us with images of the antipodean Sydney suburbs. With the visually fabulous *The Goddess of 1967* (2000), the whole film records an Australian trip from a suburb, across a bushland, to the underground mines of Lightning Ridge. With *Letters to Ali* (2004), a 6,000 kilometer trip is documented. When interviewed for *The Goddess of 1967*, Law expressed her sentiment toward the outback: "I found it really scary. The landscape seemed so vast and inhospitable; my first impression was that it was very hostile and primeval, without any feeling for the people that inhabited it."[22] Four years later, on *Letters to Ali*'s webpage, Law acknowledges, "to understand the vastness of Australia, one really has to physically travel through the land." Law admits that, with Trish and Rob Kerbi as her guides, the journey to Port Hedland became "a great enjoyment," and she was able to "have the leisure to marvel at the beauty of nature, the boundless horizon, the intense light and changing colors of the sky, the immense primeval landscape."[23] In a way, the documentary feels at times to be more about Law's marvel at Australia than a recording of Ali's ordeals. As a filmmaker known to be a "virtuoso stylist," Law seems to recognize the virtuosity of the Australian skyscape and landscape, and thus relegates her own voice to word-text, content with a digital camera, pleased to merely record, bowing to the land's awesome display of light and color.

In *Letters to Ali*, similar to her endeavored grasp of Australian cultural icons and idioms in *The Goddess of 1967*, key aspects of the political history behind mandatory detention in Australia are skipped over in Law's interview clips with Malcolm Fraser (former Prime Minister, 1975–83) and Ian MacPhee (former Immigration Minister, 1979–82). When asked about why *Letters to Ali* does not inform the viewers about the fact that it was the Labor government who introduced mandatory detention (the Keating government in 1992), Law admits, "I didn't realize mandatory detention was introduced by Labor."[24] For Clara Law, a film stylist, it is not historical or political details of Australia that convert her into identifying with the country. Her arrival in Australia is similar to Ali's—to seek a form of asylum, a sanctuary from the uncertainties of what comes after Hong Kong's 1997 handover, to seek a haven where she can contemplate the evolution of her film style, and experiment on divorcing herself from representing Chineseness. Her conversion to Australia begins when she comes to sense how the country with its unique light and color, meld with her filmic palette.

Law demonstrates her exploration in *The Goddess of 1967*'s fanciful computerized manipulations of the Australian landscape, mixing them with the technological design and beauty of the iconic 1967 Citroen DS. Her conversion turns fuller in *Letters to Ali* as she travels from Australia's green-coastal south, through the dry inland with its sudden blinding dust storms, through vast areas of red earth, to the sunny north. This traversing becomes a process of appropriation; and as the Australian topography is being digitally recorded, Law enunciates her ruminations on migration, superimposes her word-text musings onto the images, and articulates her own "rhetoric of walking."

"Walking rhetorics" is a term introduced by Michel de Certeau in his article "Walking in the City." The article stresses how people or walkers, in contrast to administrative bodies or city designers, can produce their own space by their everyday walking, transgressing the constraints imposed by the established grids of the city. De Certeau then links this walking to speech-act, to the act of writing, thus, the "rhetoric of walking." Although the article is about the urban, de Certeau's formulation helps delineate the process of Law's approach to Australia. Australia emerges as an idea of home in her *Wonton Soup* as Law deals with and mourns the disappearing Hong Kong. Then images of suburban Sydney and flashing appearances of the iconic kangaroo come forth in *Floating Life*. Law next pictures a near-surrealistic road trip through the south-eastern part of Australia vehicled by a fantastic pink Citroen. However, it is only when Law "walks" 6,000 kilometers of land in a 4–WD that she can "appropriate" Australia. As Law gets down, dusty and dirty in her journey to Port Hedland, at times unable to see as dust storms attack, she tactilely feels the land and can then "poach" images of the landscape. It is also then that she can quietly articulate her "walk," her sense of the land, her practice of Australia. At long last, with the Trish family as her guide, Clara Law has been offered her "ruby slippers" in her filming of Ali's story: she walked through the red dusty road and came to identify Oz as home.

Clara Law, ever since she began filming about migration in *The Other Half and the Other Half* (1988), has been practicing what Salman Rushdie states about the ever-favorite MGM classic, *The Wizard of Oz* (1939):

> the real secret of the ruby slippers is not that 'there's no place like home', but rather that there is no longer any such place as home: except, of course, for the home we make, or the homes that are made for us, in Oz: which is anywhere, and everywhere, except the place from which we began. (Rushdie, 57)

Clara Law has worn, and perhaps has been fixated on, her own ruby slippers and filmed about the desire for home for more than a decade. Her films with Chinese elements—*Farewell China* (1990), *Autumn Moon* (1992), and *Floating Life*—not only deal with migration and the desire for home, but also the desire for leaving. Law's films embody an anxious sense of Chineseness:[25] they evoke the possibility of a new home and also a chance to walk away from her "trouble," to escape from the fear of displacement, an ambivalent sense of identity, and the difficult process of identification. Law's *Letters to Ali* frees her from that Chineseness; it enables her to walk the red earth of Oz and marvel at "the intense light and changing colours of the sky"; it helps her locate an elsewhere from messy Chineseness. *Letters to Ali* makes filming "a journey of capturing changing lights and colours," a journey which Law says with relish, "I could rely totally on my intuition."

Documentary has never been Clara Law's genre; video has not been her favored material. Deciding on a story from the newspaper, filming without much pre-production work, Law's *Letters to Ali* breaks away from the sensibility of her previous work and emits a sense of settlement. *Letters to Ali* paradoxically leads Law away from and towards home: away from the grey and blue of the North to the light and color of the South, away from a troubling and struggling Chineseness to a settlement towards one's uprooted self. *Letters to Ali*, with its enabling video, allows Law to find a renewed sense of the filmic, and manifests home as a form of film act. And so, filming is home, filming is escape, and Clara Law has filmed her way to an elsewhere that is Oz.

Notes:

1. One can also consider Alma De Groen's work as often tackling the interplay of—to use Elizabeth Perkins' terms in her introduction to *Wicked Sisters*—rational intelligence, imaginative intelligence, and emotional intelligence. See De Groen *Wicked Sisters*, v–xii.
2. *Life After George* specifies that it is set in "a University in Melbourne"; the atmosphere evoked by the play has a Carlton, University of Melbourne ambiance. See Rayson *Life After George*, 1.
3. Elizabeth Perkins, in her introduction to *The Rivers of China*, sees in Katherine Mansfield's intricate short stories an embodiment of "the metaphysical concept of form." See De Groen *The Rivers of China*, xii.
4. An Akhmatova poem quoted in *The Woman in the Window*. See De Groen *The Woman in the Window*, 25.
5. Early details of "Follow the yellow line" and Rachel's dialogue "I want to go home!" suggest the shadow of *The Wizard of Oz* behind the play. See De Groen *The Woman in the Window*, 3.

6 De Groen cites a matrix of cultural figures and works in *The Woman in the Window*, writers and works such as Pushkin, Meyerhold, *Cherry Orchard, Anna Karenina*, etc.

7 The conservative force in *Inheritance* calls to mind figures such as Pauline Hanson, John Howard. In 2005 Hannie Rayson, in her play *Two Brothers*, further explored conservative forces in Australia by telling a story of the political lives of a pair of brothers. Many associated the play's two brothers as Peter and Tim Costello; Peter Costello served as the Treasurer in the Howard Government from 1996 to 2007.

8 Quoted from Hilary Glow's "Speaking Truth to Power: Hannie Rayson's 'Inheritance'." See Rayson *Inheritance*, xi.

9 This article's Tracey Moffatt segment and Jane Campion segment are a reworking of parts of the paper "Heat and Pleasure Down Under: *Holy Smoke* and Its Challenges." See Shen.

10 Moffatt's *Nice Coloured Girls* (1987), *Night Cries—A Rural Tragedy* (1989), *be Devil* (1993), and *Heaven* (1997, video) are available in DVD form through Ronin Films. Moffatt's work also traveled to Taiwan in August of 2001 and was exhibited at the Taipei Fine Arts Museum.

11 Catherine Summerhayes, in her "Haunting Secrets: Tracey Moffatt's *beDevil*," describes how Moffat's work tends to haunt and taunt, bewilder and bedevil in its plotting. See Summerhayes.

12 *Guapa* is a Spanish feminine term for "good looking," "cute." Moffatt used this word as the title of her 1995 black and white still photograph series, which focuses on female roller-skaters, reminiscent of those seen in US's TV roller derbies.

13 "Sensual thinking" is an Eisensteinian term Patricia Mellencamp uses to articulate the affective power of Moffatt's *Night Cries*. See Mellencamp. It is a term which I also consider to be most appropriate in explaining the emotive force in Moffatt's work in general.

14 During a conference presentation of my study of Tracey Moffatt's work, I was asked about Moffatt's use of the heavy word "tragedy" in the title of her 17–minute film. I see her word usage as a device to nudge us into an allegorical reading of the short film, calling our attention to the repressed voice within the Australian narrative, to the dark and painful experience embedded in a story set in a country where much of the land is rural, if not outright arid.

15 When words such as "assimilation" and "reconciliation" are used in the Austra-

lian context, they may point toward particular moments in Australian state policy. From the late 1930s to the mid-1960s, the forced adoption of Aboriginal children by white families, with the intention of culturally and biologically assimilating them into white society, was imposed. In order to remedy many past insensitivities, the Australian Parliament in 1991 unanimously supported the establishment of a Council for Aboriginal Reconciliation. In 2007, the Labor Government's Prime Minister Kevin Rudd delivered an apology to Indigenous Australians for the Stolen Generations.

16. Laleen Jayamanne, in her study of *Night Cries*, not only notices that the film is "glossy and breathtaking" in the way of the "big movies," but also states that it is from this good-looking film that she "learned of the harrowing history of the assimilation policy of forced adoption of Aboriginal children and what it means in terms of lived experience between a 'mother' and 'daughter'." See Jayamanne "'Love me tender, love me true, never let me go'," 4–5.

17. The articulation of landscape in Australian film, its relation to the notion of the sublime, and the link of both to the White gaze and White ethos have been explored in articles such as, "Camera Natura: Landscape in Australian Feature Films" by Ross Gibson, "White Panic or Mad Max and the Sublime" by Meaghan Morris. See Gibson and Morris.

18. "worldly, tough . . . corrupt" are characteristics *In the Cut*'s writer Susanna Moore had in mind for Malloy; Moore states that Mark Ruffalo was for her "quite an unexpected choice." See Horyn.

19. In her promotional interviews for *In the Cut*, Jane Campion repeatedly stresses her interest in exploring romantic myths, and expresses her own thoughts about self, romance, relationship, and romantic love. See Fuller and Campion.

20. This article's Sue Brooks segment and Clara Law segment are a reworking of the paper "Filming One's Way Home: Clara Law's Letters to Oz." See Shen.

21. Graeme Turner begins his "Redefining the Nation: From Purity to Hybridity" with an examination of the hybridity of ethnicities in Australian films, and then concentrates on an analysis of the cultural significance and impact of the multiracial band Yothu Yindi and their 1991 song "Treaty." See Turner.

22. From Palace Film webpage, no longer available on the Internet.

23. <http://www.letterstoali.com>.

24. From World Socialist Web Site: <http://wsws.org/articles/2004/oct2004/law2-o11_prn.shtml>.

25. Rai Jones, in his "Framing Strategies: *Floating Life* and the Limits of 'Australian

Cinema'," focuses on Clara Law's *Floating Life*, does a fine analysis of how the film performs the anxiety of Chineseness in the national, transnational, and diasporic condition, and highlights the strategy employed to manage this anxiety. See Jones.

References:

Alemany-Galway, Mary. "Postmodern Feminism in *The Piano.*" *Womenvison: Women and the Moving Image in Australia.* Ed. Lisa French. Melbourne: Damned Publishing, 2003. 309–22. Print.

Campion, Jane. "Directors Speak: *In the Cut.*" *IF* (Nov 2003): 14–15, 14. Print.

Cancela, Lorena. "Feminist Filmmaking without Vanity or Sentimentality: An Interview with Sue Brooks." *Cineaste* (Spring 2004): 18–21. Print.

Caputo, Raffaele and Geoff Burton, eds. *Second Take: Australian Film-makers Talk.* St. Leonards NSW: Allen & Unwin, 1999. Print.

Collins, Felicity. "*Japanese Story*: A Shift of Heart." *Senses of Cinema* 29 (2003) Web. <http://www.sensesofcinema.com/contents/03/29/japanese story.html>.

——. *Australian Cinema After Mabo.* Cambridge: Cambridge UP, 2004. Print.

de Certeau, Michel. "Walking in the City." Trans. Steven Rendall. *The Practice of Everyday Life.* Berkeley: U of California Press, 1984. 102–18. Print.

De Groen, Alma. *The Rivers of China.* Sydney: Currency Press, 1987. Print.

——. *The Woman in the Window.* Sydney: Currency Press, 1998. Print.

——. *Wicked Sisters.* Sydney: Currency Press, 2003. Print.

Francke, Lizzie. "Interview: Jane Campion, Dangerous Liaisons." *Sight and Sound* 13.11 (Nov. 2003): 19. Print.

Fuller, Graham. "Sex and Self-Danger." *Sight and Sound* 13.11 (Nov. 2003): 16–19. Print.

Gibson, Ross. "Camera Natura: Landscape in Australian Feature Films." *Australian Cultural Studies: A Reader.* Eds. John Frow & Meaghan Morrise. Urbana & Chicago: U of Illinois Press, 1993. 209–21. Print.

Horyn, Cathy. "Becoming a Thoughtful Woman's Idea of a Leading Man." *New York Times Magazine* (9 Nov 2003): 72–75. Print.

Jayamanne, Laleen. "'Love me tender, love me true, never let me go': A Sri Lankan Reading of Tracey Moffatt's *Night Cries*: A Rural Tragedy." *Toward Cinema and Its Double: Cross-Cultural Mimes.* Bloomington & Indianapolis: Indiana

UP, 2001. 3–12. Print.
Jones, Rai. "Framing Strategies: *Floating Life* and the Limits of 'Australian Cinema'." *Womenvision: Women and the Moving Image in Australia*. Ed. Lisa French. Melbourne: Damned Publishing, 2003. 253–65. Print.
Martin, Adrian. "Moffatt Makes the Big Time." *Artlink* 16.4 (1996): 13–15. Print.
Mellencamp, Patricia. "An Empirical Avant-Garde: Laleen Jayamanne and Tracey Moffatt." *Fugitive Images: From Photography to Video*. Ed. Patrice Petro. Bloomington: Indiana UP, 1995. 173–95. Print.
Moffatt, Tracey. *17 December 2003–29 February. 2004*. (exhibition booklet put out by Museum of Contemporary Art, Sydney, Australia). Print.
Morris, Meaghan. "White Panic or Mad Max and the Sublime." *Trajectories: Inter-Asia Cultural Studies*. Ed. Kuan-Hsing Chen. London: Routledge, 1998. 239–62. Print.
Murphy, Kathleen. "Jane Campion's Passage to India." *Film Comment* (Jan/Feb 2000): 30–36. Print.
Polan, Dana. *Jane Campion*. London: BFI, 2001. Print.
Rayson, Hannie. *Life After George*. Sydney: Currency Press, 2000. Print.
——. *Inheritance*. Sydney: Currency Press, 2003. Print.
Rushdie, Salman. *The Wizard of Oz*. London: BFI, 1992. Print.
Shen, Shiao-Ying. "Filming One's Way Home: Clara Law's Letters to Oz." *Chinese Women's Cinema: Transnational Contexts*. Ed. Lingzhen Wang. New York: Columbia UP, 2011. 347–367. Print.
——. "Heat and Pleasure Down Under: *Holy Smoke* and Its Challenges." *Tamkang Review* 35.3–4 (2005): 61–85. Print.
Summerhayes, Catherine. "Haunting Secrets: Tracey Moffatt's *bedevil*." *Film Quarterly* 58.1 (Fall 2004): 14–24. Print.
Turner, Graeme. "Redefining the Nation: From Purity to Hybridity." *Making It National: Nationalism and Australian Popular Culture*. Sydney: Allen & Unwin, 1994. 119–39. Print.

"Subjectivity" and "Otherness" in Australian Literature

Yasue ARIMITSU
Doshisha University, Japan

Introduction

V.S. Naipaul, the British-Indian writer from the Republic of Trinidad and Tobago in the West Indies said in an interview: "The world is full of excitement for me. Reality is always changing. It changes constantly and the writer has to find new ways of capturing the reality." (Naipaul, 107) Naipaul thus suggests that the reality of the world is not solid but changeable, and the concept of "individual self" or "identity" which is closely related to culture is always changing. Therefore, writers should always create new ways of writing according to these changes. Naipaul also remarks: " . . . there is no tradition of form that comes with language. The tradition that does come, from the nineteenth century, is a moral one. It is the striving after truth, the hard look at the world, and its effect is subversive" (Naipaul, 110).

It is not unusual for writers to be living and working outside their home countries these days and their works are often more highly evaluated in their adopted countries than in their original countries. Readers sometimes read these novels without knowing the writers' nationalities or ethnicities; they might be Asian, Anglo-Celtic, or sometimes indigenous writers. It seems quite difficult to identify their nationalities or ethnicities, particularly in the case of works written in English. Australian literature, for example, is read on a worldwide scale by going across by traversing national, cultural, and ethnic borders, since Australian writers usually write in English.

Even works written in other languages, however, can also quite easily go beyond language borders by means of translation and such works can be read widely outside their authors' countries of birth as well. Works by the Japanese author Haruki Murakami, for example, are read widely in translation outside Japan although they were all written in Japanese. In addition, recently in Japan, some writers whose first languages are not Japanese have written novels in Japanese and been awarded prestigious Japanese prizes.[1] Literature thus now does not necessarily represent any particular ethnicity, culture, and language within the frame of a nation, but shares them with people throughout the world.

It has been recognized that modern fiction has developed based around the "modern self" which reflects a nation based on one ethnicity, culture, and language. However, since the world has been globalized and a nation is now not necessarily based on one ethnicity, one culture, and one language, contemporary literature does not always follow the frame-work of modern literature. As a result, it seems to be quite difficult to identify the authors' "individual self," "identity," or "subjectivity" in their works and it is accordingly difficult to identify the "others" as well. This tendency shows that the representation of "subjectivity" in fiction has been changing and the distinction between the "individual self" and "others" has blurred and, as a result, the function of fiction has been undergoing a transformation in the age of multiculturalism and globalization.

In this paper, I intend to investigate how the concept of "subjectivity" represented in contemporary fiction has been transforming in relation to the "others." I am dealing with three Australian writers, because Australia has long been recognized as a multicultural nation since it has continued to accept a considerable number of immigrants from all over the world: Europe, Asia, South and North America and so on. Australian society has been, in fact, at the forefront of a developing cultural globalization. The writers I will consider are: Helen Demidenko (Darville) with a Ukrainian-Anglo-Celtic background, B. Wongar (Sreten Bozic) with Serbian-Aboriginal background, and Nam Le with a Vietnamese background. These three writers transformed their ethnicities although their purposes and manners are all different and also the social responses to these writers are different as well. I would like to compare them with respect to the ways they represent their "subjectivity" and "otherness" in their writing, and clarify the meaning of "subjectivity" in literary works in the multicultural and globalizing world.

Author and Cultural Authenticity

In recent years, writers from non-English speaking backgrounds have made a great contribution to the literary scene in Australia. Their work has extended the scope of concerns and the subject matter of Australian writing in many significant ways. The work of such writers has enjoyed some vogue, particularly in academic circles where multicultural studies in literature, sociology, and history have proved highly attractive fields of study and research. Also their work has been highly evaluated by judges in literary awards commissions. The judges seem to imply that works produced by migrant writers are much more interesting than works penned by writers of Anglo-Celtic origin.

In the mid-1990s, Helen Demidenko, a young Australian writer, created a sensation in the Australian literary scene by writing a novel under the guise of a Ukrainian immigrant. Her novel, *The Hand that Signed the Paper* (Demidenko, 1995), was awarded several important Australian literary prizes. However, the book became controversial, because the author's real identity was revealed; Helen Demidenko, it transpired, was not a Ukrainian immigrant after all but an Australian of Anglo-Saxon ancestry by the name of Helen Darville. The resulting debate highlighted the division between literary critics who focused on text itself and commentators who emphasized the ideological power of politics or history. It seems that the run of prizes for Demidenko's novel largely reflected the triumph of the critics' aesthetic criteria, but it is also assumed that the author's ethnic identity weighed with the judges more heavily than it should have. The judges were themselves judged to have leaned toward "political correctness." The Demidenko Affair thus demonstrated the very complex political, sociological and cultural involvement in literary works in multicultural Australia.

The reason why this novel was given the Miles Franklin Award, the most prestigious Australian literary award, was that it is a novel about the migrant experience and it seemed to seize the high ground in contemporary Australian fiction, in contrast to fiction about the more vapid aspects of Australian life. This comment implies that works written by migrant writers are much more interesting than works written by writers of Anglo-Celtic origin.

If the judges awarded the prize to this novel because of the author's ethnic cultural background, it was because they appear to have expected the author to be a representative of the particular cultural group she belonged to and to convey historical events her family had personally experienced in the past. In other words, they read this work as a piece of sociological data rather than a piece of literary work. If this is true, then the judges accordingly respect the author's cultural authenticity. If the reader reads her novel, for example, as a work which introduces us to an unknown, exotic culture and the writer's cultural authenticity subsequently turns out to be suspicious, the novel may then run the risk of being considered a fake. For this reason, works created by writers from non-English speaking backgrounds tended to be treated not as literature per se but as pieces of native information from the specific cultural group that the author is taken to represent.

Helen Darville, as a mainstream Anglo-Celtic Australian, needed something new, something different in the multicultural society and attempted to change her identity. She had never experienced being part of a minority and as a result she had to disguise herself as a Ukrainian writer and provide some Ukrainian family story to Australian readers. Her novel was widely read and became very popular because she presented a new phase of Australian society which is very different from the single layer Anglo-Celtic society.

However, after the author's real identity was revealed, Australian readers' attitude changed and the judges of the literary award changed their attitude as well: "It was the words that mattered, not her identity" (Jody, Totaro and Tyshing, 125). The judges emphasized that the novel was awarded the prize for its literary quality, not for the author's ethnic identity. This seems to contradict what they had said previously: the work is "about the migrant experience," "incorporating into the cultural memory first-hand experience of the major historical events of the century" (Kramer, Michehell, Heseltine, and Kitson, 19). It seems that

Demidenko's disguise of her identity confused the judges' criteria for their evaluation of her novel as well as her readers. The readers could not accept her fake identity.

The readers who could not accept Demikenko's behavior expect fiction to be written by a person whose ethnicity is equal to her writing. This is the framework of modern literature; a literary work represents the nation, culture, and language of the author. It seems that, for readers, cultural authenticity is very important, and the value of a literary work should be decided by its cultural authenticity and, as a result, they were not able to approve Demidenko's novel because it was a fake. Therefore, works by writers from non-English speaking backgrounds tend to be treated not as literature but as pieces of native information from the specific cultural group that the author represents. This reading position, as Sneja Gunew points out, "is a way of reducing and trivializing a creative text into a piece of sociological data" (Gunew, 59).

It is very important for minority writers such as indigenous Australians to write about their own culture. However, multicultural society has a tendency to force writers into a sociological viewpoint so that ethnic writers are only rewarded if they focus on writing narratives about their own culture. This is limiting and encourages exoticism. At the time Helen Demidenko appeared in Australia, the attitudes of judges of literary awards towards Demidenko's work probably came from their obsession with the ideas of cultural essentialism and political correctness. In these attitudes we can observe a framework of difference between "Australians" and "others," the "mainstream" and the "periphery," or "subjectivity" and "other," and there were no possibilities for Australians to cross the borders of ethnicity and culture even though the national border was transcended.

Indigenous Writings in a Multicultural Society

The two cases of Demidenko and Wongar are similar in that they disguise a minority author although the former is a disguise from an Anglo-Celtic Australian to a Ukrainian, from mainstream to non-mainstream while the latter is from a European immigrant to an Aboriginal, that is, from non-mainstream to non-mainstream. In Demidenko's case, I examined how literary works by authors with non-English speaking background are evaluated in multicultural Australia, and the nature of cultural authenticity in Australian literature. In Wongar's case, I intend to focus on why B. Wongar, a Serbian immigrant from the former Yugoslavia, had to disguise himself as an Aboriginal, and what Aboriginal cultural authenticity and Aboriginal identity in Australian literature are.

The question is, why did Wongar publish his books under the name of B. Wongar, an Aboriginal name. Wongar was a Serbian immigrant called Sreten Bozic. Bozic was born after his father came to Australia from Yugoslavia in the 1930s and but his father later took him back to Yugoslavia. He came back to Australia after his father died and went to the Northern Territory and lived there with Aboriginal people. He then married an Aboriginal woman and had two children. He had a hard life in a reservation with his family because he himself was white, and also suffered from land destruction by the mining companies. His wife and children died because they drank contaminated water. He deeply deplored what was happening in the land they were living in and as a result decided to write books to protest against the Australian government. He wrote about the fact that many Aboriginal people were killed because of the nuclear weapons testing and published a trilogy of nuclear protest. He also held an exhibition of his own photographs of the nuclear testing areas. He protested against the Australian government as an Aboriginal. This was the reason why he wrote books under an Aboriginal name.

When Bozic started to write in the 1970s, it was at a time when Australian society remained largely divided between the Anglo-Celtic centre and the non-Anglo-Celtic periphery and it goes without saying that the immigrants from Yugoslavia found themselves on the periphery. At that time, as is well known, non-Anglo-Celtic immigrants were discriminated against and it was almost impossible for them to achieve much success in Australia. If they wanted to publish books, they could not obtain any support from publishers or the government. Bozic in fact applied for grants from the government many times but without success (Drewe, 5). At that time, however, Aboriginal writers such as Kath Walker (later Oodgeroo Noonuccal) and Jack Davis[2] were well known as writers and activists in civil rights movements in Australia and widely accepted by Australians. It was, therefore, quite natural for Bozic to think that he could attract more people if he wrote under an Aboriginal name rather than his real European name.

However, things did not go as he expected. Wongar's books did not sell well in Australia, although they were successful overseas. An editor of Angus and Robertson, one of the major publishers in Australia, tried to publish Wongar's books in the late 1980s, because one of his works, *The Track to Bralgu*, had sold 250,000 copies worldwide. Unfortunately, however, this plan did not work; Australians had become rather suspicious about his works. Thus his books did not sell well despite the popularity of Aboriginal literature in the 1980s. There is a tendency for most white readers not to trust Aboriginal stories written by non-Aboriginal writers such as Europeans like Wongar, because these books were not considered culturally authentic. For many Australian readers, the authenticity of literary works depends on their writers' cultural identity. For these readers the book is not worth considering if its cultural authenticity is suspicious. This might be the major reason why Wongar's books did not sell well in Australia.

This reminds us of the case of Demidenko. Australian readers rejected Demidenko's work for many reasons, but it can be assumed that the writer's identity was one of the major reasons. Readers did not trust her book because it was written not by a Ukrainian, but by the Anglo-Celtic Helen Darville. Given that a writer's identity is very important for readers, and greatly affects the value they may attach to the books written by that author, it is fair to ask whether books by non-Aboriginal or non-Ukrainian authors about Aboriginal or Ukrainian culture become worthless.

Gunew has again argued that "we are confronted with the question of distinguishing between our readings of "Wongar" and our reading of the texts which bear his proper name." She pointed out that:

> Australia [has] the practice of bracketing Aboriginal writing in English with the ethnic writings. Here surely is a prime illustration to the fact that we have an unmarked monocultural norm of Anglo-Australia and measure against this the "others," the ethnic groups, the prevailing logic being that the Anglo-Celts do not participate in "ethnicity." That the Aborigines should be classed with the minority others is surely one of the most outrageous of the dispossessions they have suffered as a colonized people.
>
> (Gunew, 267)

Gunew thus claims that Australian society in the mid-1990s was still polarized according to an Anglo-Celtic/non-Anglo-Celtic binary division. Although Australia declared itself to be a multicultural society, it was almost impossible for non-Anglo-Celtic writers to cross the socio-ethnic border, and if they did, they crossed two borders as a writer. In Wongar's case, first, the border between Serbian and Anglo-Celtic identities when he wrote in English, and second, the border between Serbian and Aboriginal identities.

Unlike Demidenko's case, however, Wongar's case was not a disguise of Aboriginal identity. He gained an identity of Aboriginality, as Michael Connor and David Matthew argue:

> His [Wongar's] work consistently threads the problematic of his own identity into the narrative, collapsing the outside/inside distinction. Throughout all the stories there are figured shadowy characters who are, or have been, European, but become increasingly identified with dispossessed peoples."
>
> (Connor and Matthew, 715)

Since he actually lived as an Aboriginal, Wongar's identity was transformed from being a European to being an Aboriginal. Thus it can be said that the border between his texts and his own identity disappeared.

If you question the issue of cultural authenticity, you never fail to turn to the issue of cultural essentialism, just in the case of Demidenko, because the author is always expected to provide culturally, socially, and politically authentic information to readers. Moreover, those who pay a great deal of attention to literary works by authors with ethnic identities are usually Australians of Anglo-Celtic origin and are not migrants of other ethnicities. Because of this trend, many literary awards go to writers with apparent ethnic identities like Helen Demidenko. This illustrates that Australian literature is still controlled by Anglo-Australians; the judges seem to lean towards "political correctness." As a result, Australian cultural identity cannot yet really be defined as multiple representations, but is still in a binary structure of Anglo-Celtic and non-Anglo-Celtic.

What Wongar achieved through his works by transforming his identity from European to Aboriginal is the creation of a completely different world which is neither purely Aboriginal nor purely Serbian, but something completely new, namely a mixed identity born of two cultures: European and Australian. What he has done then is to bring European culture closer to Australia and vice versa and thereby create a completely intellectual, hybrid world. This is a work of diaspora, a mixture of multiple cultures; one that is symbolic of identity in this postcolonial period.

Through these two cases, it seems that in this globalizing world, it is almost impossible for any culture to remain as it is; any society is bound to undergo continual change as it mixes with others. In any multicultural society, the important thing is not to question cultural authenticity but to pay attention to what will come from the mixture or fusion of different cultures within it. Naipaul again, in his interview, remarks:

> . . . The novelists who came after used the novel form to get at truths the essay couldn't get at—truth about society and mental status, for instance.
>
> The great novels of the nineteenth century still have this quality of truth; and part of their excitement is that the writers

can be felt to be writing about certain things for the first time. They were not versions of what had gone before, and novels like them cannot be done again. Form and content go together. You cannot simply pour new experience or new material into an old form; that is not only to write somebody else's book all over again; it is also to falsify the material. The traditional novel never really existed; good work was always new. Reality always has to be captured. Methods will change as the world changes. Everyone will find his own way. (Naipaul, 110)

Thus, cultural and literal identity never remains static and unchanged, but will always keep mutating into something new and in this process will always create new possibilities. It could be said that in the multicultural, globalized society of the present, it is almost impossible for us to discern an author's cultural identity or authenticity from the narrative in her/his literary works.

Transformation of Subjectivity[3]

In terms of the postcolonial viewpoint, Nam Le is surely an ethnic writer if ethnicity[4] implies a minority group in Australia. Ethnic groups in Australia consist of immigrants from non-English speaking and non-white countries throughout the world, as well as the Australian indigenous people. Ethnic writers write from the periphery to the Anglo-Celtic mainstream of Australian society. However, Nam Le has complicated ethnic, cultural and national backgrounds. Being Australian, his ethnicity is Vietnamese by birth, but his first language is English because he was brought up in Australia. As a result, he culturally belongs to Australia rather than to Vietnam. As Caylo-Baradi remarks, Nam Le has thus "a sort of double-consciousness, being ethnic and non-ethnic" (Caylo-Baradi, 2009). His "double-consciousness" might be interpreted as a "hybrid figure," which seems to assume blending of his cultural and ethnic identities.

It has been recognized that modern fiction has developed around the "modern self" which was based on a single nation, ethnicity, culture and language but Nam Le is not such a case. Taking his nationality, ethnicity, as well as his cultural and language backgrounds into consideration, he is neither a representative modern writer nor a representative national writer of Australia. As Caylo-Baradi again remarks, it is possible to say that, because of this, in *The Boat*, Nam Le is attempting, just as Wongar was, to do something very new, something different from modern national fiction and reflect his own multiple selves (Le, 2008).

Most readers of *The Boat* associate the title and its author's name with "boat people" from Vietnam and they expect to read about the author's experiences as a refugee from Vietnam because many immigrant writers have written of their own experiences as immigrants and become renowned as "immigrant writers." They have become very popular as their writing usually gives readers new Australian perspectives. However, Nam Le's book was contrary to expectations. Two of the book's stories surely have something to do with refugees from Vietnam but they are not based on the author's experiences. The book seems to declare something about the author's principles of writing fiction as a contemporary writer, not as an immigrant writer who writes from the periphery, but as a writer blending national, ethnic and cultural backgrounds.

In this globalizing world, there are many writers who left their home countries just as Nam Le and Wongar did and became writers in their new countries. These writers' viewpoints do not necessarily represent one nation, one culture and one ethnicity. This fact shows that the concept of "subjectivity" or "individual self" is no longer based on a single nation, culture or ethnicity. If modern "subjectivity" or the "individual self" has been transformed in this way, then, modern fiction, which has been considered as representing the "modern individual self" has been transformed into something else. It seems that in *The Boat*, Nam Le is trying to show this transformation by focusing on the concept of "subjectivity." In this part, I intend to examine the transformation of concepts of "subjectivity" and "individual self" and as a result, how the concept of "fiction" has been transformed in *The Boat*.

It is quite surprising to read so many favourable comments on Nam Le's first literary work *The Boat*.[5] This makes a stark contrast with the previous two cases. Australian readers rejected Demidenko and Wongar's novels because their authors' ethnic identities were not authentic. This leads to the question of who the writer Nam Le is. He was born in 1978 in Vietnam, and his parents escaped from there, taking him with them when he was only three months old. His family stayed in a refugee camp in Malaysia for a while and then arrived in Australia as boat people and settled in Australia. After that he was educated in Australia, graduated from Melbourne University and worked as a lawyer for a while in Melbourne. However, he found himself unsuited to being a lawyer, and decided to become a writer. He went to the United States, joined the Iowa Writers' Workshop[6] and obtained a Master of Arts in Creative Writing. After that he worked as an editor for the journal, *Harvard Review*, and started to write. In 2008, he returned to Australia, but now he lives in England.

Some of the immigrants who came to Australia in the 1970s and 1980s started to write literary works. When they wrote, they tended to write about their experiences in their home countries as well as in Australia. They were usually well received by readers as they provided them with new perspectives on Australian literature, which had been mostly dominated by Anglo-Celtic writers who were mainly the descendants of settlers from the British Isles. The new literature attracted Australian readers who had never experienced life as refugees outside Australia. Australian writers with ethnic backgrounds thus established their peripheral positions in Australian literature. They were often called postcolonial writers and their works were treated as postcolonial literature.

Many publishing companies were very much interested in them and published their works and they sometimes had commercial success. In addition, publication of Indigenous writing increased in the 1960s in Australia. In 2008, Nam Le made his debut and his book, a collection of short stories, was published. His name had a strong impact on the publisher as it reminds readers of the Vietnamese, and the title of the book, *The Boat*, particularly reminded them of boat people. Thus, there were no reasons not to pay attention to his book and publish it. When they actually did so, it was a great success.

Nam Le's success, however, was not because he was an ethnic writer or because his writing was about his experiences as a refugee. The seven short stories neither reflect the author's ethnicity nor are they about the author's experiences, although the settings of two stories are in Vietnam or about Vietnamese people. The remaining five stories have nothing to do with the author's ethnicity, personal experiences or even his times.

The characters in the stories do not have anything at all in common with the author himself. Ironically, this is one of the important reasons why his book attracted the attention of so many readers as well as critics.

Nam Le, as a writer, portrayed a number of people who have no single cultural, ethnic or national identities and sometimes even cross gender borders without any difficulties. Cate Kennedy, in her interview with him, says that:

> Longer than the average Australian short story by several thousand words, each one differs so markedly from the others in style, voice and setting that you are left shaking your head in admiration that they could all have been written by the same author.
>
> (Kennedy, 2008)

The collection of short stories takes readers to Colombia, Hiroshima, New York, Tehran, and Australia. Each story has its own setting, spread widely in terms of time and space. His stories are perfect fiction which floats in an imaginary time and place.

When asked about the book, he said: "When I was writing the stories there was that sense of wanting to do different things but I think that can be attributed to the fact that I was reading so much at the time" (Cunningham, 135). It would have been quite natural for him to think that if he had an ethnic background, he might be expected to write about a story which reflects his own ethnicity. Particularly if you live in a country with a significant number of immigrants such as Australia, the United States and Canada and you are a writer with an ethnic background, your works tend to be read as something to do with your ethnicity. In this case, readers usually read the books as if they were the stories the authors experienced in their real lives.

However, if authors are writing fiction, that is not the way to write it. What Nam Le was interested in was to write something which transcended the national, ethnic, cultural as well as religious boundaries, instead of writing something reflecting his own background. He wrote stories with settings in places all over the world, regardless of whether West or East. He says about himself as a writer:

> I was born in Vietnam, raised in Australia, currently live in the US, and have mucked around through chunks of Europe, South America and Asia. It's not a stretch to say that the reasons why I travel and why I write or read are similar: to see other things, other places, situations and people, *through other eyes*.
>
> (Kennedy, 2008) (Italics mine)

Nam Le attempted to write from various viewpoints, transcending a single focused viewpoint, and look at others through "other eyes." If he is trying to do something new in his fiction, he is trying to transcend his own "subjectivity."

In postcolonial literature, if postcolonial writers are writing about others, they are looking at "others" from their viewpoints, not from "others' viewpoint." For postcolonial writers, it was very important to retrieve their own independent "subjectivity" after the colonial period as the colonized were deprived of their culture, language, and sometimes religion. The colonized people were released from the colonial structure and in order to rectify this, they had to establish their own independent "subjectivity." And this was the way to establish a kind of national or cultural identity.

As multiculturalism proceeded in Australian society, ethnic and cultural blending occurred through marriages between the former colonizers and colonized and also between Anglo-Celtic Australians and immigrants from different countries. As a result, national, ethnic and cultural borders between the former colonizers and colonized became blurred, and national, ethnic and cultural identities were intertwined and sometimes even disappeared. This takes place not only through biological blending but also through other forms of blending as in the case of Nam Le. Nam Le has multiple identities within himself; his ethnicity is Vietnamese, his nationality is Australian, and it is difficult for him to tell which his real identity is. For him there is no clear border between "self" and "others" in the framework of postcolonialism.

Nam Le feels full of inconsistencies in himself as a writer and as an immigrant; he is surely one of the "others," apart from the mainstream, but at the same time he is no longer Vietnamese as he does not have any connection with Vietnam. For him, national, ethnic and cultural identities hinder him from writing fiction if these ethnic and cultural identities are the original base for modern literature. It might be said that he became interested in a totally different way to write. In the collection of short stories *The Boat*, with the exception of two stories which come at the beginning and at the end, he attempts to write stories to transcend his national, cultural and ethnic identities. When he writes such stories, he becomes stateless; for him the border or confrontation between "himself" and "others" has disappeared, and this means that he does not have any definite "subjectivity" of his own.

Nam Le is a writer with multiple identities. Therefore, it is possible for him to write various fictional characters with a variety of national, ethnic and cultural identities. In so doing, he writes characters not as "others" but as part of himself; he shares something with these characters in spite of their different ethnic, national and cultural identities. For him, it might be impossible to write fiction from only a single viewpoint, and there are no borders between himself and "others" in creating fictional characters.

I will take up three stories to examine the author's way of presenting characters, whose national, ethnic and cultural identities seem not to be directly related to his own backgrounds, and investigate how their "subjectivities" are presented in the stories. One is "Hiroshima" and the second is "Halflead Bay," and the third is "Tehran Calling," because "Hiroshima" is a special story for Japanese readers, "Halflead Bay" is meaningful for Australians, and the third story "Tehran Calling" is a very complicated story; the central character is an American, but the setting of the story is both in America and Iran, and the story takes readers to a different place, space and even to a different world of religion.

The central character of "Hiroshima" is a little girl in the early years of primary school. This is a first-person narrative, and Japanese life during World War II is depicted from the viewpoint of a young girl.

> Sumi, you will be safe there. Through the rain I see the big *torii* archway to the Shrine on Miyajima Island. It floats like a red spirit above the water. Forgive me, I will not run from danger, says Big Sister. Water drips down from the rim of her air-raid hood. You taught me the story of the son of Ieyasu—honour won in youth grows with age. You fought the enemy in Manchuria. I am not a child. I know the way of Bushido and I will fight like you. (Le, 201)

It is very clear that Nam Le did detailed research on Japanese lifestyles, particularly at the time of the war. His research was not only on Japanese people's life but also great Japanese historical figures, and in addition, he has a thorough knowledge of Japanese militarism. However, he did not make the little girl understand or judge the meaning of war or comment on the sense of values during the war. She, of course, does not know that they are going to be bombed very soon.

One of the features of this story is the contrast between what is said and what is not. What is not said in this story stimulates readers' curiosity and imagination and it promotes better understanding of the situation of atomic bomb victims in Hiroshima. Regarding what is not said in "Hiroshima," the author allows his characters to float in fantasy, illusion or dreams, and in so doing, he creates characters with no strong will power or "subjectivities." He uses the stream of consciousness technique, and shows the characters' "sub-conscious." These methods have an effect on readers; they are not at all informed about what is actually happening, although they know the atomic bomb is going to destroy the whole city of Hiroshima and its people. The readers are deeply moved by the story because the most important event is not actually mentioned here. The author makes the reader imagine the disastrous experience of the atomic bomb simply through the young and innocent girl's stream of consciousness. The first person narrative can be most effective in making readers believe in "fantasy," "illusion," "dreams," as well as "stream of consciousness."

"Halflead Bay" makes a stark contrast with "Hiroshima." The story is about the everyday affairs of a commonplace Australian family depicted through the eyes of a high school boy. The boy's mother is suffering from a fatal disease, his father caring for his wife, and he himself is distressed by a clumsy relationship with his girlfriend and a love-hate relationship with his brother.

The big difference between "Halflead Bay" and "Hiroshima" is the author's relationship with the backdrops of the story. In terms of ethnicity, Australians are "others" to Nam Le, but his nationality is Australian, and in this sense, Australians are not "others" to him. Therefore, the characters in this work do not seem to be strangers to him, and it is important to note that this is not a first-person account. The author does not depend on memories, fantasies, illusions or stream of consciousness in portraying characters, but uses realism instead.

> Michael, face tracked with mud, went to pick up his bike, steered it around. He wheeled it close by them. Jamie held fast to his dad's shoulder. At the edge of the clearing his dad stopped, turned, as though to kiss him on the head, then said, 'You're okay, son.' They started the long walk home. (Le, 185)

The characters are all clearly depicted; the story itself is very realistic and easy to follow, and it ends with hope and happiness, although, on the other hand, the main character of "Hiroshima" is floating in her memories, imagination and sub-consciousness, and the way of presenting the central character's "subjectivity" was ambiguous. As a result, it seems that the distance between the viewpoint of the author and the viewpoints of the characters is closer than those of the other story "Hiroshima." "Subjectivity" is more clearly visible in this story than in the others.

In this collection of short stories, the author wrote about several characters with different backgrounds crossing national, ethnic, cultural as well as religious borders. However, for the author, crossing borders does not simply mean to present multiple identities and to fuse them but to remove "subjectivity" from himself as well as his characters. The author can become anybody by removing his "subjectivity," and can create any characters disconnected from his own identity. Most of his characters, therefore, do not act of their own accord because they are not based on a national, ethnic and cultural background. As a result, the author lets the characters float in their memories, illusions, and dreams as well as sub-consciousness. The author tends to keep a distance between himself and his characters.

The "subjectivity" of the character in "Tehran Calling" differs from that of "Halflead Bay" and the other stories. The central character, Sarah, is an American but the setting of the story is both in America and Iran. The structure of the story is very complicated, because Sarah is an American girl, who is one of the "others" for the author, and there is another character, Parvin, an Iranian girl, who is also one of the "others" for Sarah as well as the author. The story takes readers to a different place, space and even to a different world of religion.

Sarah meets Parvin when she comes to the United States to study and they become very good friends and they understand each other very well.

> She'd calibrated herself to be above average in all the average ways: running down the hours, the feasible commitments, the ready consolations of work and sleep. She'd built her life, elegantly, around convention—conventional aspiration, conventional success—and was continually astounded that no one saw through the artifice—no one recognized Sarah Middleton as all

falsework and nothing within. Only Parvin had sensed this, she felt, and back in college had accepted Sarah into her friendship with as few questions as she wanted asked of her. It wasn't that they weren't intimate, or equal—more that Sarah, by nature, found it easiest to fall in with her, and had always been grateful for it. (242–243)

Sarah thinks that they understand each other very well without asking much about them. Sarah even thinks that Parvin understands her better than Americans.

However, when Sarah visits Parvin in Tehran after Parvin returned home, Sarah comes to know that Parvin is not what Sarah knew in the United States. Sarah thinks she and Parvin understand each other very well only when they are in America. In Tehran, Sarah realizes that there are many things about Parvin which she does not understand. Parvin turns out to be a sort of stranger to Sarah. She is deeply shocked at this fact.

When Nam Le wrote this story, it seems that he wanted to cross ethnic, national and cultural borders without restraint, but at the same time, he wanted to show the difficulty of understanding other people, other cultures and religions. This fact shows that Sarah thinks she understands Parvin when she is in her own country but not in Parvin's country. This exactly means that Sarah understands Parvin only in Sarah's viewpoint, not in Parvin's. "Subjectivity" in this story is on Sarah's side, and it is almost impossible for her to become one of other people.

Nam Le, in writing this story, seems to be quite successful in crossing borders of nationalities, ethnicities and cultures as he controls his characters according to their backgrounds. However, he is not quite successful in fusing them, mixing them as is described in the scene where the two characters cannot reach mutual understanding. While Sarah understands Parvin only from her viewpoint and not from Parvin's viewpoint, it is not clear enough whether or not Parvin understands Sarah from Sarah's viewpoint. It might only be an illusion on the part of Sarah that she felt they fully understood each other.

In *The Boat*, the author wrote about several characters who have different national, ethnic cultural as well as religious backgrounds crossing all these borders. However, for the author, crossing borders is not just to present multiple identities and to fuse them but to remove "subjectivity" from himself as well as his characters. The author can be anybody by removing his "subjectivity," and can create any characters disconnected with the author's identity. Most of his characters, therefore, do not act of their own accord because they are not based on a national, ethnic and cultural background. As a result, the author lets the characters float in their memories, illusions, dreams as well as sub-consciousness. The author tends to keep distances between himself and his characters.

Nam Le with blended identities creates characters with various identities without depending on his national, ethnic, cultural identities but depending on something else, something represented by illusion, fantasy and sub-consciousness. Nam Le describes human reality not within the limits of national, ethnic and cultural identities but beyond them. He uses fantasies, dreams and sub-consciousness, which are not solid or stable, but changeable, floating and ambiguous. The first and the last stories support this fact: although these two stories reflect a Vietnamese background, they are not really related to Nam Le's identity, since although Nam Le is ethnically Vietnamese, nationally and culturally he is not.

Conclusion

Nam Le describes human reality unbounded by the limits of national, ethnic and cultural identities. He creates characters with various identities with no reflection of his own identities but depending on something else, something beyond national, ethnic and cultural identities. He thus uses fantasies, dreams and sub-consciousness, which are not solid or stable, but changeable, floating and ambiguous.

Demidenko's novel represents cultural identity not as a plural or multiple but as a binary structure of non-Anglo-Australia against Anglo-Australia. It is possible to argue that Helen Darville, an Anglo-Australian writer, wrote this novel deliberately for Anglo-Australian readers. This is a major difference between the work of Demidenko and the works of Wongar and Nam Le. Wongar and Nam Le reflect more complicated ethnic and cultural backgrounds and transcend the binary structure of multicultural society, with Wongar attempting to blend plural ethnicities and cultures, and Nam Le to cross over ethnicities and cultures and remove conventional "subjectivity" or "individual self" to create new ways of writing fiction in the multicultural and globalizing world. The two writers thus demonstrate the fact that the reality of the world is not solid but changeable, and the concept of "individual self," or "subjectivity," which is closely related to culture is not solid or fixed but always changing.

Notes:

1 Yang Yi was awarded Akutawaga Prize in 2012 for her *Tokiga Nijimu Asa* (Tokyo: Bungeishunju, 2008).
2 Jack Davis (1917–2000) was a well known Aboriginal poet and playwright. He was also a noted political activist for indigenous rights.
3 This part is based on the paper, "Nam Le's *The Boat*: A Reflection of Multiple Selves," Michael Kenneally, Rhona Richman Kenneally, and Wolfgang Zach (eds.), *Literatures in English: New Ethical, Cultural, and Transnational Perspectives* (Stauffenburg Verlag, 2014).
4 Ethnicity is a term "that has been increasingly used since the 1960s to account for human variation in terms of culture, tradition, language, social pattern and ancestry, rather than the discredited genetically determined biological types. . . . Indeed, few terms are used in such a variety of ways that with such a variety of definitions—Isajaw (1974) deals with twenty-seven definitions of ethnicity in the United States alone. . . . The term "ethnicity" however, really only achieves wide currency when these "national" groups find themselves as minority within a larger national grouping, as occurs on the aftermath of colonization, either through immigration to settle colonies such as USA, Canada, Australia, New Zealand, or by the migration of colonized peoples to the colonizing centre." Bill Ashcroft, G. Griffiths and Helen Tiffin, *Key Concepts in Post-Colonial Studies* (London: Routledge, 1998), 80–84.
5 Richard Lea, *Guardian*, November 11 (2008), Online Posting, <http://www.guardian.co.uk/books/2008/nov/11/dylan-thomas-prize>.
Michiko Kakutani, *The New York Times*, May 13, 2008, Online Posting, <http://www.nytimes.com/2008/05/13/books/13kaku.html>.
Andrew Riemer, *Sydney Morning Herald*, June 20, 2008, Online Posting, <http://www.smh.com.au/news/book-reviews/the-boat>.
6 The Iowa Writers' Workshop at The University of Iowa is a two-year residency program which culminates in the submission of a creative thesis (a novel, a collection of stories, or a book of poetry) and the awarding of a Master of Fine Arts degree, 2007, University of Iowa, Online Posting, < http://www.uiowa.edu/~iww/ >.

References:

Caylo-Baradi, Michael. "Nam Le: To Write or Not to Write an Ethnic Story," *PopMatters*, March 6 (2009): Online Posting. <http://popmatters.com/pm/tools/print/66821>.

Connor, M. and Matthew, D. "In the Tracks of the Reader, In the Tracks of B. Wongar." *Meanjin* 48(4) (1989): 715. Print.

Cunningham, Sophie. "The Friction Zone: Sophie Cunningham Talks to Nam Le." *Meanjin* 68 (1) (2009): 135. Print.

Demidenko, Helen. *The Hand that Signed the Paper*. Sydney:Allen & Unwin, 1995.

Drewe, Robert. "Solved: The Great B. Wongar Mystery." *The Bulletin Literary Supplement* 21 (1981): 2–7. Print.

Gunew, Sneja. "Culture, Gender and the Author-Function." *Southern Review* 20(3) (1987): 261–270. Print.

Jost, J, G. Totaro & C. Tyshing, eds. *The Demidenko File*. Ringwood: Penguin Books Australia. 1996. Print.

Kennedy, Cate. "Nam Le, Interviewed by Cate Kennedy." *Readings*. May 29 (2008): Online Posting. <http://www.readings.com.au/interview/nam-le>.

Kramer, L., A. Michhell, H. Heseltine, and J. Kitson. "'The Judges Report, Miles Franklin Award,' Taken from an extract in Forum on the Demidenko Controversy." *Australian Book Review*. August (1995): 19. Print.

Le, Nam. *The Boat*. Camberwell: Penguin Books. 2008. Print.

Naipaul, V.S. "V.S. Naipaul with Alistair Niven." *Writing Across Worlds: Contemporary Writers Talk*. Ed. Susheila Nasta. New York: Routledge, 2004. 102–112. Print.

Expanding Horizons:
Australian Television and Globalization in the 1950s–1970s[1]

Kate DARIAN-SMITH
University of Melbourne, Australia

In 1971, nine-year-old Dmetri Kakmi emigrated with his family from a small and remote Aegean island in Turkey to the city of Melbourne in Australia. Overwhelmed by the "thrumming megalopolis," Kakmi recalled:

> As my brain ticked away at the problem of how to locate myself within the city's sprawl, I realized that the answer had stared me in the face all along: television.
> This fabulous invention was no mere abstraction. For someone who was used to living in his head, the images presented on screen were more real and contained more truth than reality. Discovering television when I did shifted the ground beneath my feet and influenced my life . . . . (Kakmi, 22)

For migrants to Australia in the middle to late decades of the twentieth century, especially those coming from non-English speaking countries of origin, the everyday presence of television was to be influential in assisting their settlement into their host country. The content of early

Australian television, consisting of a mixture of locally produced and imported programs, the latter primarily from Britain and the United States, alongside advertisements and news, was to play a significant if not formally acknowledged role in introducing new arrivals to the values and nuances of the "Australian way of life" (White). For Kakmi, who as a child avidly viewed Australian and American children's television every afternoon after school, television programs also offered insight into ways of living that existed well beyond the boundaries of his family and neighbourhood in either his previous life in Turkey or his current one in Australia. From an adult perspective, Kakmi has reflected that 'the act of watching [television] expanded, rather than limited, my worldview" (23).

In the post-Second World War period, the expanding horizons offered through television programming were, of course, not just viewed by new migrants but by the Australian population as a whole. Television was introduced into Australia in 1956. This was a good decade after full-scale commercial television had become widely available in Britain and the United States, and half a decade after it was available in Japan; but it also preceded the introduction of television to many other nations, including parts of Europe and Asia. From its inception, television was to have a profound influence on how Australian audiences viewed their own society but also on how they became more conscious of some aspects of a wider world, including that of their immediate Asian region. Taking an historical perspective, this chapter will examine some of those links between television programming, consumption and globalization as these existed from the 1950s to the 1970s, in the period prior to the late-twentieth century introduction of newer media and communication technologies, such as the internet or the personal computer.

In its initial decades, television—then a new media form, but one that is now classified as old media—did play an important role in both assisting in the settlement of new migrants and in maintaining a connection with a distant "homeland" for diasporic communities in Australia. The mass migration schemes of the 1950s through to the 1970s were accompanied by the gradual dismantling of the White Australia Policy, and its racial restrictions on immigrants, and the rise of multiculturalism as an official policy under the Labor government of Gough Whitlam (1972–75). The Australian population grew at an astonishing rate from 1945, rising by 40 per cent to reach 10.5 million in the 1961 census (Tavan, 109). This growth was the result of the increased birthrate of the post-war "baby boom," and an open immigration scheme with government assistance for many migrants from Britain and other select countries, including for certain periods with migrants from Italy and Greece. Although Australia remained predominately British in the origin of its people and its cultural practices, the arrival of substantial numbers of migrants from central and southern Europe, and by the 1970s from the Middle East and then Vietnam meant that there were discernible ethnic changes amongst its population (see Jupp).

From the late 1950s, Australian, British and American programs predominated on television, and their collective emphasis was on the histories and cultures of the English-speaking world. Despite some national variations in language or lifestyle or geographic location, there were more similarities than differences between local Australian programs, and British or American imported programs, in their presentation of social and cultural values. The shifting ethnic demographics of Australian television audiences were not reflected on the screen, with the casting of television personalities and actors in locally produced television dramas generally limited to those of Anglo-Australian backgrounds. In this sense, the depictions of Australian society on television were selective rather than representative of Australia's increasing cultural diversity; this was a situation that was to be ongoing and led to a number of government and industry reports (Bell, Goodall, May, Nugent *et al*).

Drawing on a larger study of the history of television and immigration, and an associated oral history project, this chapter traces some ways that early television in Australia contributed to the formation of a national and international sense of belonging among its diversifying audiences.[2] Although there have been studies about the vital role of the media in creating a sense of identity and belonging for migrants to Australia during the late twentieth century (Cunningham and Sinclair), little scholarly consideration has been given to what television meant for migrants in earlier decades. I will investigate that gap, and also examine the impact of television in assisting migrants in the process of settlement in their new country. I will also look at the influence in Australia of two popular television dramas about Asian societies as illustrative of the relationship between the Australian television and the globalizing flows of media production, circulation and consumption within and across the Asia-Pacific region.

Television Comes to Australia

Television is both a ubiquitous and powerful presence in everyday life. The content of its programs have deeply penetrated our cultural imaginations, and program scheduling and viewing practices serve to structure our daily routines and behaviours. The intimacy of television as a domestic medium situates it within the mundane and subliminal "ordinariness" of our lives, in ways that may be perceived to be outside the realm of national history and historical processes. Yet, from its technologies to its programming production and audience reception, television is an historical phenomenon, and the complexities of television culture can only be understood within their historical moment.

This history of television is relatively short in Australia. Television initially was transmitted in 1956 in the two largest cities of Sydney and Melbourne, just in time for the viewing of the Olympic Games in the latter. The Melbourne Olympics were a key moment for postwar Australia, and by hosting the world's famed sporting competition it was felt that Australia was taking a rightfully elevated position in international affairs and would continue to develop its global influence (Davison). The presence in Melbourne of journalists and film crews from around the world to cover the Olympic Games spurred the necessity that domestic audiences have television access to an event that was simultaneously international in its reach and participation and national in its execution and location.

However, it was not until 1959 that television was available in the other state capitals of Adelaide, Perth, Brisbane and Hobart. Access to a clear transmission signal was to take much longer still in non-metropolitan areas. Almost everyone's first experience of television was communal, as it was watched with friends, relatives and neighbours in both private homes and domestic spaces prior to the mass-purchasing of individual sets. However, by the early 1960s Australians had embraced the new technology with great enthusiasm, and, where there was reception, the vast majority of homes either purchased or rented a television set.

Television not only shaped the cultural and social lives of Australians in the late 1950s and 1960s, but also was highly influential as a source of news and general perspectives on the wider world. In the aftermath of World War II, Australia's international relations had shifted. The war had forced Australians to be alert to their geographical location in the Asia-Pacific and the implication of this for trade, communications and regional security alliances. Percy Spender, Minister for External Affairs in the Liberal government of Robert Menzies that came to power in 1949, argued that in the post-war period Australia's "centre of gravity" in the world had shifted to its immediate region. This was evident in the Australian support for regional economic development, including investment in such schemes as the Colombo Plan, which sponsored international students from the Asia-Pacific to study in Australia in order to gain new skills to take back to their own countries. In a speech given on March 1950 to the Federal Parliament, Spender laid out the foundations of a new Australian foreign policy that was to dominate the following decades:

> We are indeed a Pacific power. . . . We have similar interests, strategic and otherwise, in the South and South-East Asian area. No nation can escape its geography. . . . Even though our cultural ties have and will remain predominantly with Europe . . . we live side by side with the countries of South and South East Asia and we desire to be on good neighbour terms with them.
> (*Commonwealth Parliamentary Debates*, 621–40)

Australia's cultural ties with America, not to mention links related to trade and security, had also strengthened in the aftermath of World War II. Spender was instrumental in Australia being a signatory to the ANZUS Treaty with New Zealand and the United States in 1951. This signaled a significant shift in Australia's alliance with the United States, and both nations shared a fear of Communism and believed in the "domino principle"—that is, that the 1949 Communist victory in China would lead to communist insurgency throughout South-East Asia. The Cold War and conflict in Korea and Vietnam underpinned Australia's relationship with America in the 1950s and 1960s. So too did the expansion of economic and cultural interactions between the two nations, which was evident in the influence of American popular culture.

In Australia, the introduction of television in 1956 coincided with an unprecedented period of industrial expansion and high export prices. By the second half of the 1950s, this had resulted in increased prosperity for most Australians. The increased birth-rate and the surge in population due to migration led to substantial growth in infrastructure, commercial and industrial facilities, and new housing within Australian cities. These factors contributed to the spread of suburbia, with its accompanying and highly prevalent social aspirations for home ownership—ideally of a family dwelling on a quarter-acre block. This meant that television also arrived in tandem with, and indeed spurred on, the rise of a modern consumer society in Australia which was centered on the home and the suburb. The availability of television, and its visualization of modern life, both facilitated and reflected what Michelle Arrow has called "Australia's transformation from a production to a consumption-oriented society" (144).

Aligned to both the growth of suburbia and consumerism in Australia's postwar decades was a renewed and politicized interest in the role of the family within the community, and by extension within the nation (Lewi and Nichols). In this context, the impact of television on family interactions, and on the social and physical development of children, was to be widely and vigorously debated by educators, politicians and the media. Just as children and teenagers were to become new market-segments for the promotion and expansion of consumer goods in the 1950s, they also comprised audience categories for television programs and advertising. Television was criticized by some as a deterrent to a stable and productive family life—through both the family practice of watching television and the unwelcome influences conveyed through the content of its programming (Darian-Smith, Spigel). But it was more generally seen as a positive force on the recreational and educational activities of Australians, and as a visual extension of the programs that had been popular on radio: news, sports, variety and games shows and serial dramas.

Programming on Australian television during the 1950s and 1960s was dominated by imported shows from the United States and United Kingdom, continuing a practice of imported films shown in the cinema that dated back to the 1920s. Just as Hollywood films had often been criticized in Australia for contributing to the "Americanization" of Australian culture—a phenomenon seen as undesirable by many intellectuals and commentators—so too were American television programs. In the very first years of Australian television, programs from the United States predominated on the commercial channels, and it was largely the national broadcaster, the Australian Broadcasting Commission (ABC), that provided some British and Australian alternatives. Early television programming served to highlight the significance of imported global programs over those that were made within Australia. At the same time, television advertising was often so highly localized to its regional town or city that it also functioned to obscure the place of a national identity formed through television content. By the 1960s, this was to change with increased Australian content on commercial channels as well and subsequent decades witnessed a growing sense of 'the nation' in television programming across all genres, from drama to news to comedy (Turner).

One sizeable constituency that has not been addressed in the existing histories of early television in Australia has been that of its migrant groups: the initial postwar intake of European refugees, the next wave of migrants from the Mediterranean and the large numbers of arrivals from Britain. Indeed, the existing scholarship on the history of television has also ignored what we might think of as a prehistory of television viewing, including the prior knowledge and experiences of television that migrants brought to Australia from other countries.

Migration, Memory and Television

The arrival of television to Australia from 1956 coincided with massive demographic and economic change across the nation. The rapid expansion of industry and infrastructure, and high prices for primary exports, meant that by the late 1950s Australians had entered a "long boom" of economic prosperity. The mass-scale migration scheme launched by the Australian government after World War II brought waves of migrants from Central, Northern and Southern Europe to work in the expanding manufacturing sector. While the largest groups of migrants came from Britain, by the early 1960s there were substantial communities of new arrivals from non-English-speaking countries, particularly Italy and Greece.

For British migrants—many of them sponsored on the "Ten Pound Pom" immigration scheme—television in Australia offered a mix of familiar and unfamiliar programming. Alistair Thomson's study of British women who moved to Australia during the 1960s and 1970s reveals that for these migrants the screening of British television shows provided a "potent" link with their family and friends left behind (121). In a letter "home" to England, one woman wrote of the American as well as British programs that were available: "television out here is like the BBC in England. We have *Mickey Mouse, Z Cars, and Sooty and Sweep, Steptoe and Son*" (40).

The exchange of views and news about British television serials expressed through correspondence between British migrants in Australia and their families in Britain maintained a sense of connection, collapsing the distance between the two nations. The popularity in Australia of British television serials such as *Coronation Street* also meant that British migrants could share their expert knowledge of contemporary British life with Australian neighbours and friends (Thomson, 121).

But television also offered British migrants—as well as other new arrivals—a point of entry into Australian cultural life and sensibilities. The language and gags of local advertisements and variety programs, as well as television personalities such as Melbourne's Graham Kennedy and Bert Newton, highlighted a particular sense of Australian values and humour (Thomson, 121).

Australian news, and current affairs programs, also aired political and social issues of national importance, and in doing so conveyed to new migrants a sense of Australia's place within the wider world and the key domestic issues and political concerns. In the 1950s and 1960s, Australia's international links focused on the strengthening of diplomatic, security and economic ties with the United States, and the continued maintenance of the long-established relationship with Britain. Indeed, the enthusiasm of Australians for Britain can be seen in the extraordinary responses in 1954 to the Royal Tour of Queen Elizabeth II throughout the continent. Once television commenced, the national broadcaster ABC television screened much British content. The popularity of the British royal family extended to non-British migrants, who equated this with a demonstration of Australian nationalism. For instance, the Verins family, Latvian migrants who had arrived in Australia in 1951 and made a home in the inner Melbourne suburb of Brunswick, bought their first television in time for the televised royal wedding of Princess Margaret in 1960—an event greeted with much interest and excitement in Australia (Irene V and Nina V).

In comparison with the United Kingdom and the United States—where television broadcasting commenced in the 1930s, was interrupted by World War II and resumed in the 1940s—early Australian television was relatively undeveloped in its initial production and transmission technologies. Television was certainly not a novelty for migrants from Britain. It is likely that the majority had direct experience of television ownership within their immediate or extended family prior to migration, and in any case British migrants were well acquainted with domestic television etiquette.

Moreover, the rapid take-up of television in Australia after 1956 resulted in an initial shortfall of experienced technicians able to install and repair sets. In order to meet this shortage, skilled technicians were sought from the United Kingdom, not just to work in suburban businesses and for companies like Astor, but also to provide the knowledge in the production areas of the ABC and the commercial television studios. The Commonwealth Department of Immigration, responsible for the promotion of Australia to potential migrants, documented profiles of successful British migrants who worked as technicians within the growing television industry (National Archives of Australia). Such profiles were intended not only to lure other potential British migrants to Australia, but also to address the shortage of skills needed in a modern media industry.

In contrast, while British migrants "knew" television, those from Italy and Greece in the 1950s and 1960s generally had little or no direct experience of its domestic viewing prior to their migration to Australia. Television broadcasting, which operated under state ownership, began in Italy in 1954 but with a reach that was expensive and limited. The 1950s were a period of reconstruction and social and industrial transformation in Italy, with millions of Italians moving within the country: from Southern to Northern Italy, from small villages to large cities, and from occupations in agriculture to those in industry. In this environment, and contrary to the expectations of intellectuals and politicians, television was to become an immediate success. At first, for most Italians, television sets were too expensive for the average family. This meant that television was viewed in a public setting such as in bars and cafes, in cinemas and even in churches. By 1958, there were around thirty people watching every television set in Italy, attesting to the communal nature of the medium (Buonanno, 15). In 1961, a second channel, also state owned, was introduced and by the mid-1960s television in Italy had a nationwide audience, with sets increasingly purchased for the home. In a country still characterized by a high level of illiteracy, with a traditionally low circulation of the daily press (among the lowest in the world) and irregularity of school attendance, television quickly became the most widespread form of media in Italy.

Image 1:
Mr Angelo Revello, a migrant from Turin, Italy, at work editing a film for Australian television. NAA: A12111, 1/1958/16/72, 1958.

In Greece, the situation was somewhat different. With an agricultural economy and a long period of rebuilding after World War II, television was not introduced until 1966, with limited viewing under a state-owned monopoly. In 1968, a second channel, under the control of the military junta government, was opened. However, television transmission remained unavailable to many Greeks living outside Athens and other cities and towns until the early 1980s. In Greece as in Italy, television was also initially often watched in a communal setting, and took time to become commonplace in individual homes.

Therefore, of the hundreds of thousands of Italians and Greeks who came to Australia, the vast majority had never owned a television set and many had never seen television—or if they had, it was in a bar or other public place. For those with little education, the image-based nature of television proved a boon to learning English, whether this was a conscious acquisition or not. This was particularly effective for children, including those of pre-school age, whose parents spoke no English in the family home. Nicholas V recalled that when his family came from Greece, he was aged five and had several younger siblings. English was learnt once they started school, but "having another source of English [on television] would have assisted immensely." There was also incentive to learn English so as to follow and enjoy the plotlines of favourite television series (Nicholas V).

The influence of the American and British accents that were heard in imported television programs on the acquisition of English language by migrant children and adults is difficult to assess. Francesco G, who migrated from Sicily as an adult, and had some education and an interest in politics, recalled that he taught himself English by listening to the broadcast of Australian parliamentary debates on ABC radio. He found that the images on television were a distraction, and that he did not have to concentrate so hard to understand the thrust of the story (Francesco G).

For schoolboy migrant Dmetri Kakmi, "television was no mere entertainment" but "a benevolent tool of the government, an electronic medium that inducted new arrivals in local rituals and habits." He reasoned that, "if one acted on the lessons imparted by the all-knowing box, one would assimilate very quickly" (23).

Ownership of a television set could serve as an important marker of social and economic status. Maria's family, who came from Calabria and settled in western Sydney, had saved up carefully for a television. Once they were accustomed to the television as a feature in the lounge room, it was turned on constantly, and competed with the highly voluble Italian family conversations (Maria G). Armanda also recalled that her father drew television into a family narrative of migrant success in Australia, often telling the story that he was "the first in the street to buy a television." She remembered that many Italian migrants always had their set turned on in the family home, and watched it for lengthy periods and often in social groups (Armanda S). For Nicholas V's large Greek family, a television set was a prized possession:

> We didn't have a television until we moved into our own house in North Richmond and that's only because my siblings and I would go and watch TV in the showroom of a furniture shop in the main street, in Victoria Street. . . . And then one of my aunts who lived nearby and was newly married bought a TV, and we used to go and watch it there. So eventually my father bought a cheap secondhand TV that didn't work very well to the point that one of us used to have to sit underneath a table to balance the floor so it would get good reception. Eventually he bought a [new] TV on hire purchase, a Thorn Atlas, which he paid off over a number of months or years. That took pride of place in our house. (Nicholas V)

The parents of Nicholas V never watched television or listened to the radio during the 1950s and 1960s, although they did play records and had an active social life within community and ethnic organizations. This was because they both worked long hours in factories, leaving little time to settle in front of the television or to learn more than rudimentary English. Indeed, prior to 1964 only 2.5 per cent of all media content in

Australia could be broadcast in languages other than English, which then required an immediate translation to avoid complaints to the Australian Broadcasting Control Board (Ang, Hawkins and Dabboussy, 15).

Gradually, however, the rules were relaxed and both commercial and community radio played a part in the development of "ethnic" content. By the 1970s, the official policy of multiculturalism spurred the establishment by the Whitlam government of two Ethnic Australia radio stations, which provided news and other programs in languages other than English as a service for migrant communities. The popularity of the broadcasting of Ethnic Radio led to the establishment of the Special Broadcasting Service (SBS), which by the 1980s was responsible for the development of a multilingual television network that was to expand television's reach even further into Australian homes (Ang, Hawkins and Dabboussy, 8–9). The impact of television programming, including drama serials, variety shows and news services, in languages other than English was to have a remarkable effect on some migrants. "When I first saw SBS television," wrote Italian-Australian Anna Maria Dell'oso, "I cried . . . because I felt some part of my story had finally been officially placed into the jigsaw puzzle that is society, Australian life . . . in the language of my parents" (O'Regan, 121).

The Samurai and *Kung Fu*: Imagining Asian Cultures

Television served as a bridge between Australia and the wider world in the 1950s and 1960s, but this was a world that was generally restricted to the United States and Britain if it is to be measured by the origin and the content of the programming that was available. News services and documentaries were more expansive in their coverage of other countries and international events, but overall were Anglicized in their outlook. In this last part of this chapter, I explore how television was to play a unique and often forgotten role in providing insight into the histories and cultures of Asia and more specifically into the past cultures of Japan and China.

My focus is on high-rating popular television serial dramas, rather than movies or other one-off documentary programs. It is certainly worth noting, however, that during the 1950s to 1970s there was a steady stream of highly patriotic American and British movies shown on Australian television—often on Saturday afternoon or evening—about World War II, including war in the Pacific theatre. Such movies provided Australians with dramatic representations of an historical event that was still very present within living memory, and often incorporated negative images of Asia and Asians (and in particular the Japanese) in this wartime context.

In 1964, in an extraordinary venture, the commercial Channel 9 broadcast *The Samurai*, the first Japanese television serial ever shown in Australia. Made by Senkosha Productions, with its Australian screening dubbed with American-accented English, *The Samurai* depicted the exploits of a roving samurai warrior in eighteenth-century Japan, with story arcs including lost treasure, ninja warfare and much horse-riding and sword-fighting. It was to prove an unexpected success, despite residual anti-Japanese sentiment in Australia in the aftermath of World War II. The drama was particularly popular with "five- to fourteen-year-olds," and was screened at the weekday prime slot of 5.30 p.m. so that it could be viewed after the school day (A. *Australian Women's Weekly*). By 1965, *The Samurai* had become Channel 9's most successful children's television program, even surpassing the popular The Mickey Mouse Club, which was imported from the United States.

The surprise hit of *The Samurai* was to generate the first visit to Australia by a Japanese "celebrity" in the postwar decades. In the summer of 1965–66, its star, the Japanese actor Ose Koichi, toured Sydney and Melbourne where he appeared in a sold-out stage show based on the series that was held at the Sydney Stadium and Melbourne's Festival Hall (B. *Australian Women's Weekly*). Around 7,000 people, including many children and teenagers aged between 9–14 years, were dressed as ninjas when they greeted Koichi at Essendon Airport in Melbourne. This huge crowd of fans was estimated to be a larger than the screaming throng who had welcomed the Beatles when they flew in to Melbourne on their 1964 tour (Sinigaglia).

Image 2:
Australian Women's Weekly, Wednesday 18 August 1965, p. 16. Reproduced with the permission of Bauer Media Limited. National Library of Australia.

The televised screening of The Samurai series was not without controversy. In 1965, the *Daily Mirror* newspaper reported that Rex Morgan, the headmaster of a Sydney preparatory school, Pittwater House, had "banned Shintaro [swap] cards and any association with the cult." Denying he was a "right-wing reactionary," Morgan asserted:

> I question the mental health of a nation which permits its schoolchildren to be exposed to the current cult of Japanese sadism and cruelty in the guise of a TV hero. I should have thought we had enough of this sort of thing during the war without glorifying such attitudes by the present TV representation. . . . This type of programme is producing sick, soft and unmanly attitudes in Australian society. (A. *Daily Mirror*)

A *Daily Mirror* reader was quick to defend the values of *The Samurai*:

> I am the father of three boys from 4 to 7½ years. The three of them watch the show as well as myself. All of us are attracted by the beauty of the art direction, camera work and general presentation of the series which is a fairly honest portrayal of life in early Japan. To see my boys running, jumping and only very occasionally standing still in emulation of the physical feats of the good or bad, seems quite the reverse of soft and unmanly.
> (B. *Daily Mirror*)

This debate about *The Samurai* is illustrative of the complexities of the histories of the early years of television in Australia, and in particular illustrates the ways in which television influenced audiences to appreciate both Asian cultures and the nation's geographical place in the region. With the escalation of Australia's role in the Vietnam War, South-East Asia was to appear regularly in television news. There is certainly more research to be done on how Australians learnt about their region through news of the Vietnam War, which was more heavily censored in Australia by the government than in the United States (Anderson).

In the period of the Cold War during the 1950s and 1960s, China also was depicted to Australians primarily through the news. By the 1970s, however, images of an historic and culturally rich China came for the first time to Australian television with the screening of the highly popular American television series *Kung Fu*. This series was made between 1972 and 1975, and starred the actor David Carradine. His character was the Shaolin monk Kwai Chang Caine, the orphaned son of an American father and Chinese mother who had met in mid-nineteenth century China. Trained as a Shaolin priest and martial arts expert, Kwai Chang Caine was forced to flee China after killing the Chinese emperor's nephew. The series covered his exploits as a fugitive in the Old West of the United States, where he searched for his American relatives. Regular flashbacks in each episode to Kwai Chang Caine's training in the monastery in China were to emphasize the mental and spiritual power of the kung fu style of martial arts.

These flashbacks also provided the audience with images of China as a place and of Chinese culture, although both were relegated to a mystical past that bore little resemblance to contemporary China and its communist government. There was, however, an attempt by the creators to present the China of *Kung Fu* as an authentic re-enactment of an historic China. It was alleged that the American writer/creator of the series, Ed Spielman, had studied Mandarin and spent long periods of time researching kung fu in New York's Chinatown.

The popularity of the *Kung Fu* television series in Australia echoed other developments in popular culture during the 1970s. The attraction of the drama was influenced by the growing audiences for Hong Kong cinema, and the mounting fascination in the West with the physical and spiritual dimensions of Asian martial arts. As with *The Samurai*, older children and teenagers comprised a sizeable segment of the audience for *Kung Fu*—and through its American values, transposed onto a China of long-ago, these young Australians came to imagine and interact with an imaginative sense of Asia and its peoples.

By the mid-1960s, television was becoming a firm and dominant presence in the daily routines of work, school and leisure for Australians. Apart from a brief initial period, television was watched and understood in the private realm of the home and the family. It coexisted with older media forms such as radio or the cinema, but was beginning to eclipse these in terms of influence. The physical replacement of the radio set with the television as the central recreational feature of the lounge room was symbolic of this shift.

Moreover, the content of television programs in the 1960s and 1970s, and its power as a visual media, was absorbed in varying and diverse ways into the imaginative and cultural regimes of adults and children. In this way, the stories of imported television serial-dramas such as *The Samurai* and *Kung Fu* increasingly both challenged and affirmed ideas about national values and Australia's place in the world—including in the Asia-Pacific region. By the 1980s, SBS television was purchasing programs from many overseas nations, primarily in Europe but also in Asia. In the 1990s, the ABC and even the commercial television stations were seeking to be more engaged with Australia's Asia-Pacific region in terms of news coverage and some documentaries, though it proved difficult to shift the Anglophone focus of drama programs. By the 2000s, extraordinary changes to both media technologies and Australia's population—the largest non-English language spoken at home in the recent 2011 Census was Mandarin—has meant that there are new ways that diasporic communities interact with their home and host countries with, and bypassing, conventional television (Australian Bureau of Statistics).

Conclusion

My purpose here has been to sketch out an important historical dimension to the history of television within the broader cultural history of Australia as a global and globalizing society. In the 1950s to 1970s, television was to play a key role in the material, emotional and imaginative regimes of Australian viewers and their relationship with both national and international events, places and peoples. For recent migrants, television's imported content sometimes offered comfort and familiarity through it images and news of their past home and this was a situation commonly experienced by those who had come to Australia from Britain. Those who arrived from non-English speaking countries, including the thousands of migrants from Greece and Italy in the postwar decades, found that through television they would be informed, whether consciously or not, about the language, cultures and values of Australia as these were depicted in news, variety and current affairs programs as well as locally produced dramas.

But all Australians, whether migrant or locally born, would learn about the United States and Britain through programming imported from those two great international powers. They could also learn about an idea—if less a reality—of Japan and China through imported television drama serials. Television programs such as *The Samurai* and *Kung Fu* were extraordinarily popular, especially with younger audiences, and perhaps part of that appeal was that the positive representation of Japanese or Chinese cultures bore little resemblance to the images of the Asian region that appeared on news broadcasts. In these ways, the "expanding horizons" provided by television in the early decades of its transmission were multiple and complex, contributing to how Australian audiences imagined and understood their nation, as well as the wider world.

Notes:

1 This is a revised version of a paper first presented at the Australian Studies Regional Symposium (Asia-Pacific), Australian Studies Association of Japan, held at Doshisha University, Kyoto, in September 2012. It draws on some material from Darian-Smith and Hamilton.
2 Further research on television and migration is ongoing, and is funded by the Australian Research Council: LP150100202 "Migration, Cultural Diversity and Television: Reflecting Modern Australia" from 2016–2018. I am also grateful to the University of Melbourne and Museum Victoria for initial funding under the McCoy Seed Grants in 2014.

References:

Anderson, Fay. "The 'Uncensored Televsion War'? Memories and Experiences of the Australian Coverage of the Vietnam War." *Remembering Television: Histories, Technologies, Memories*. Ed. Kate Darian-Smith and Sue Turnbull. Newcastle upon Tyne: Cambridge Scholars Publishing, 2012. 210–227. Print.

Ang, Ien, Gay Hawkins, and Larissa Dabboussy, eds. *The SBS Story: The Challenge of Cultural Diversity*. Sydney: UNSW Press, 2008. Print.

Arrow, Michelle. "16 September 1956: 'It's Here, At Last!' The Introduction of Television into Australia." *Turning Points in Australian History*. Eds. Martin Crotty and David Roberts. Sydney: UNSW Press, 2009. 143–56. Print.

Australian Bureau of Statistics. "Reflecting a Nation: Stories from the 2011 Census, 2012–2013." Cat. No. 2701.0, (2013). Print.

Australian Women's Weekly A. 27 July (1965). Print.

Australian Women's Weekly B. 12 January (1966). Print.

Bell, Philip. *Multicultural Australia in the media: a report to the Office of Multicultural Affairs*. Canberra: Dept. of Prime Minister and Cabinet, Office of Multicultural Affairs, 1993. Print.

Buonanno, Milly. *The Age of Television: Experiences and Theories*. Bristol: Intellect, 2008. Print.

Commonwealth Parliamentary Debates. Vol. 206. 9 March (1950): 621–40. Print.

Cunningham, Stuart, and John Sinclair, eds. *Floating Lives: The Media and Asian Diasporas*. Lanham, MD: Rowman & Littlefield, 2001.

Daily Mirror (Sydney) A. 14 December 1965. Print.

Daily Mirror (Sydney) B. 23 December 1965. Print.

Darian-Smith, Kate, and Paula Hamilton. "Part of the Family: Australian Histories of Television, Migration and Memory." *Remembering Television: Histories, Technologies, Memories*. Eds. Kate Darian-Smith and Sue Turnbull. Newcastle upon Tyne: Cambridge Scholars Publishing, 2012. 30–51. Print.

Darian-Smith, Kate. "Children, Families and Nation in 1950s Australia." *Child's Play: Dorothy Howard and the Folklore of Australian Children*. Eds. Kate Darian-Smith and June Factor. Musiam Vctoria, 2005. 19–40. Print.

Davison, Graeme. "Welcoming the world: The 1956 Olympic games and the representation of Melbourne." *Australian Historical Studies*, vol. 27, no 109. (1997) 64–76. Print.

G, Francesco. Interview with Paula Hamilton. 12 March 2011.

G, Maria. Interview with Paula Hamilton. 12 March 2011.

Goodall, Heather. *Racism, Cultural Pluralism and the Media: A report to the Office of Multicultural Affairs*. Canberra: Dept. of Prime Minister and Cabinet, Office of Multicultural Affairs, 1990. Print.

Jupp, James. *From White Australia to Woomera: The Story of Australian Immigration*. Melbourne: Cambridge University Press, 1997. Print.

Kakmi, Dmetri. "Night of the Living Wog." *Joyful Strains: Making Australia Home*. Ed. Kent MacCarter and Ali Lemer. Melbourne: Affirm Press, 2013. 19–31. Print.

Lewi, Hannah and David Nichols, eds. *Community: Building Modern Australia*. Sydney: UNSW Press, 2010. Print.

May, Harvey. *Broadcast in Colour: Cultural Diversity and Television Programming in Four Countries*, Woolloomooloo, NSW: Australian Film Commission, 2002. Print.

National Archives of Australia. "The Immigration Photographic Archive." 20 September 2015. http://www.naa.gov.au/collection/fact-sheets/fs254.aspx.

Nugent, Stephen, Milica Loncar and Kate Aisbett. *The People We See on TV: Cultural Diversity on Television*. North Sydney: Australian Broadcasting Authority, 1993. Print.

O'Regan, Tom. *Australian Television Culture*. Sydney: Allen and Unwin, 1993.

S, Armanda. Interview with Paula Hamilton. 20 March 2011. Print.

Sinigaglia, Marco. *Shintaro! The Samurai Sensation that Swept a Nation*. Documentary Film. Sydney: Screenworld, 2009. Print.

Spigel, Lynne. *Make Room for TV: Television and the Family Ideal in Postwar America*. Chicago: University of Chicago Press, 1992. Print.

Tavan, Gwenda. *The Long, Slow Death of White Australia*. Melbourne: Scribe, 2005. Print.

Thomson, Alistair. *Moving Stories: An Intimate History of Four Women Across Two Countries*. Sydney: UNSW Press, 2011. Print.

Turner, Graeme. *Making it National: Nationalism and Australian Popular Culture*. St Leonards, NSW: Allen & Unwin, 1994. Print.

V, Irene, and Nina V. Interview with Kate Darian-Smith. 7 November 2010.

V, Nicholas. Interview with Kate Darian-Smith. 3 May 2010.

White, Richard. "'The Australian Way of Life'," *Australian Historical Studies*, vol. 18, October 1979: 528–545. Print.

Multiculturalism and Media in Korean Society

Yeon LEE
Sun Moon University, Korea

1. Problem posing

Around the time when Korea held the 2002 World Cup, the number of foreign immigrants in Korea increased rapidly. It was mainly caused by rapid globalization which encouraged international marriages and migration of foreign workers and international students. Also, it could happen because digital industries and IT technologies had developed greatly and international collaboration in these areas had been facilitated.

Now, Korea has over 1,440,000 foreign immigrants and has become a multicultural society. Moreover, Korea is expected to have over 10,000,000 foreign tourists by the end of 2012, but it is also facing growing problems with this phenomena. Korea has been supporting multicultural families[1] by enacting the "Act on the Treatment of Foreigners in Korea" in May 2007 and the "Support for Multicultural Families Act" in September 2008. The main opportunity that made Korea to start such a movement was probably the visit of Hines E. Ward Jr. who is a Korean-American football player in 2006. After his visit, most Koreans changed their negative prejudice and stereotype against mixed blood people.

2. Multiculturalism and Media in Korea

2–1. Multicultural Phenomena

Korea is originally a single race nation that has traditional Confucianism. However, as international marriages increase and the number of mixed blood children increases in and around rural areas recently, it is hard to call it a homogeneous country. The marriage problems of young men in the countryside which were brought about by a scarcity of women have been the main cause of this change.

As stated above, the number of foreign residents in Korea in 2012 exceeds 1.3 million. Korea has transformed into a multicultural society with Confucianism and immigrant's culture mixed with each other, causing identity confusion to the second generation of immigrants.

Residence Status of Marriage Immigrants by Nationality
(Dec. 31, 2012, Unit : number of people)

Nationality	Total (%)	Male	Female
Total	144,681	19,650	125,031
China	64,173 (45%)	11,455	52,718
(Korean descent)	29,184	7,558	21,626
Vietnam	37,516 (25.1%)	181	37,335
Japan	11,162 (7.6%)	1,010	10,152
Philippines	8,367 (5.5%)	227	8,140
Cambodia	4,583 (3.1%)	6	4,577
Thai	2,603 (1.8%)	42	2,561
Mongolia	2,393 (1.7%)	59	2,334
United States	2,410 (1.7%)	1,808	602

Uzbekistan	1,840 (1.3%)	52	1,788
Russia	1,319 (0.9%)	70	1,249
Canada	1,158 (0.8%)	1,009	149
Nepal	840 (0.6%)	135	705
Pakistan	720 (0.5%)	669	51
Others	5,597 (3.9%)	2,927	2,670

Reference: Korea Immigration Service

Current Proportion of Marriage Immigrants by Nationality

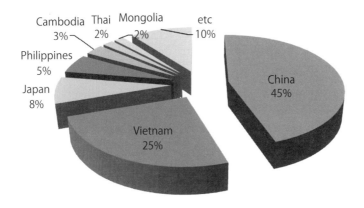

2-2. Transition of Multiculturalism in Korea

The first international marriage in Korea was the marriage between Dr. Syngman Rhee (1875–1965), first president of Korea, and an Austrian, Francesca Donner. Besides, plenty of international marriages between Americans and Koreans happened when the U.S. Army was stationed in Korea after World War Ⅱ. Unfortunately, few of those couples continued to manage a normal marriage. In the 1990s, the cityward tendency of the population aggravated the marriage problems of rural youth. This circumstance led Koreans to marry Chinese (including ethnic Koreans living in China), Filipinos, Vietnamese and others, finally leading to a multicultural age.

As mentioned above, Korea is changing from a single race country to a multicultural society. Conventionally, Korea was a Confucian society which cherishes ancestry, but it is recently seeing a sharply growing number of mixed blood children. These children have always been minorities in Korea. Mixed blood people are minorities and situated at disadvantaged circumstances in terms of politics, economy, and culture. In order to improve their situation, the government formulated several policies that promised support for multicultural families. Moreover, Sookmyung Women's University organized the "Sookmyung Institute for Multicultural Studies" in 2008 for the first time in Korea. It was followed by some other organizations that built institutions with the same purpose of multicultural studies.

(1) On 11 April 2012, the/a proportional representation candidate of the governing party, Jasmine Lee, a Filipina who became naturalized as a Korean citizen, was elected as a member of the National Assembly. She had married a Korean man but after he died, she became a government employee of the City Hall of Seoul. She continued to succeed in her job and finally became a member of the National Assembly. Lee is now participating in activities such as the "Multicultural Policies Forum" and the "Major issues of Multicultural Policies and Challenges in Legislation Forum," the main purpose of which is to promote peaceful symbiotic life between foreigners and locals.

(2) North Korean defector (defected in 1994) Cho, Myung-chul who had worked as the chief of the Education Center for Unification

was also elected as an Assembly member on 11 April 2012. He is not a mixed blood person but people like him are still considered as minorities in this multicultural society. Even though North Koreans and South Koreans share the same language, these two Koreas have been completely divided into half and hardly interacted with each other. North Korea still keeps its communism and this caused a huge gap between the two Koreas. Especially, North Koreans' accent is quite different from that of South Koreans, which makes it hard for them to communicate with each other. In fact, North Korean defectors are sometimes discriminated against in job markets if they do not change their accent. Actually, the fact that any Korean will be punished for violation of the National Security Law if he or she meets or makes contact with North Korean people is hindering communication between the defectors and South Koreans. Although it is not illegal for South Koreans to have contact with North Korean defectors since they surely acquire Korean citizenship, meeting North Koreans is still against the current law. Therefore, it is necessary to encourage the defectors to change to South Korean intonation so that they can quickly settle down in Korea.

2–3. Adaptation of Immigrants in the Multicultural Society and Media
There always exist values that people cherish in every society. Any attempt to realize the values can be considered as constituting society (Goff, 57–61). Likewise, Korea has its own values. Those include compassion, conformism, materialism, antiauthoritarianism, egalitarianism, and familism. In this environment, immigrants must fully understand those Korean values. In order to do this, they should not only conduct interpersonal communication with native Koreans as Allport argued

(1954), but also take advantage of media. In the case of interpersonal communication, it provides an opportunity to have effective communication without any misunderstanding as well as a chance to directly understand Korean society. On the other hand, while direct language usage occasionally offends other people depending on the speaker's linguistic ability, media has become an effective means of communication without such a problem.

2-3-1. Interpersonal Communication

Immigrants who frequently make contact with native Koreans or make the most of media tend to easily adapt to Korean society. Furthermore, scientific research proves that if immigrants usually only have contact with the people from their own country, they find it difficult to adapt to Korea. Allport says the reason why a person develops a distorted perception against other groups is because he did not have any direct interaction with anyone from those groups. Therefore, the more often immigrants have contact with Koreans, the less prejudice the immigrants and Koreans will have against each other.

2-3-2. Media

When immigrants are in the process of perceiving the values of Korean society, media also plays an important role. Media complement communications that immigrants usually make through interpersonal communication.

2-3-3. Immigrants and Television

Television significantly contributes to the adaptation process of immigrants. Especially, immigrants lack the ability to understand the language; yet they can still perceive social atmosphere or information through watching television. In fact, recent research regarding the actual state of immigrants' communication says immigrants are using television as the most important method in gathering information. According to the George Gerbner group's 'Cultivation Effect Theory,' as people repeatedly or prolongedly watch mass media fiction such as TV dramas, their perception of reality changes to the reality or values that are depicted on television (43–57). Concerning this theory, Hyungjin Woo and Joseph Dominic conducted a research project on international students in the U.S. who often watch talk shows. Interestingly, among the students, some students who didn't adapt to American society well enough had highly negative perceptions and attitudes toward the society (109–120). That was probably because American talk shows usually feature sex, drugs, violence, crimes, and family conflicts and those contents are often full of distortion, exaggeration, and false information. These contents of American media are considered to have led to immigrants in the U.S. developing negative perceptions and attitudes.

Likewise, immigrants in Korea can strongly recognize Korean values such as compassionism, conformism, materialism, and familism, as they keep watching media including television, radio, newspapers, and magazines. On the other hand, as the immigrants watch TV dramas or news programs that exaggerate those values, they are negatively influenced without noticing.

3. The Role of Media in a Multicultural Society

As mentioned above, media tend to reflect native values such as culture, ideology, morality, and philosophy without any censorship. In this multicultural society, media should respect foreigners and immigrants and try to harmonize them with native Koreans with the purpose of national integration. In the case of Singapore, Chinese people make up 76.7% of the national population, followed by Malaysians (14%), Indians (7.9%), and others (1.4%). Nevertheless, the government assigned city-built houses proportional to the component ratio of each race, and most people respect others' cultures in weddings, funerals, and ancestral rites. Likewise, in this age of multiculturalism, media should be able to blend different cultures with deference to difference and diversity.

With these in mind, this paper explains the role of media in a multicultural society by analyzing several examples.

3–1. Media and Cultural Conflicts

In late 2001, which was the year before the 2002 World Cup, Koreans' dog eating habit became a social issue. This was the result of cultural conflict between animal lovers who criticized the habit as animal abuse and Koreans who claimed the habit as native culture which must not be interrupted. Brigitte Bardot, a French actress, aggressively denounced the habit on a public broadcasting network named 2TV, causing a cultural conflict between Korea and France. As a result FIFA (Federation Internationale de Football Association) insisted that Korea banish the dog eating habit. Even though the Korean government got rid of signs about selling dog meat in preparation for the 1988 Seoul Olympics because of continuous external pressure, it did not let the foreign pressure interrupt the native eating habit of Korea. The Korean government argued that pet dogs are not eaten and countered that French eating habits are also cruel. Foie gras, one of the three greatest dishes in France, is made from the liver of a goose. In order to make foie gras, French people force a goose to drink an excessive amount of water, which will make its liver large enough to be cooked. The Korean government argued that this behavior is indisputably animal abuse. Also, they said that there is no reason not to eat dogs when everybody eats horses or other livestock (Lee Yeon 2003).

3–2. "Love in Asia" (KBS 1TV World)
"Love in Asia," a television show that has been aired since 1 August 2008, describes the family affection of multicultural families in Korea. The multicultural families in the show usually consist of foreign laborers or marriage based immigrants and they frankly talk about their own happy or sad experiences in Korea. The most popular and moving episode was when the reporter groups directly go to the home country of the foreign immigrants and cover their hometown family. The reporter groups are usually accompanied by the immigrants so that they can share the joy of reuniting. This episode not only emphasizes the family affection and universal humanity, but also helps Korean society to smoothly accept foreign cultures by showing the scenes where different cultures blend with each other. Korean people will start to consider foreign immigrants as real neighbors.

3–3. "Chats with Beautiful Girls" (KBS2)
"Chats with Beautiful Girls" is a program where female foreigners in Korea talk about their experiences regarding Korea, Koreans, and

Korean culture. This gives an opportunity to objectively view Korea from the perspective of foreigners. Unfortunately, the show was somewhat criticized for featuring only beautiful women and mainly focusing on their failures in Korea for the purpose of amusement. However, by listening to honest stories of foreigners in Korea which include difficult and sad experiences, Koreans get a chance to self-examine themselves and understand what multiculture really is.

Conclusion

Nowadays, media is open to global society, which allows people to discuss political, economic, and cultural issues anytime and anywhere. Also, people can understand different cultures through talking to each other without fighting to establish rights and wrongs. However, in the case of the Internet, it includes plenty of false information, requiring caution and prudence by the users.

As globalization and mass immigration continue, different ethnicities and different cultures started to coexist in one country, resulting in multiculturalism. The modern era features borderlessness between countries, which allows people to emigrate to foreign countries. Cultures also follow the emigrants, forming a different foreign cultural society in the inviting country. The inviting countries of mass immigration include increasing numbers of different cultures and races. The United States, Canada, and Australia were the most representative examples but Japan and Korea are also becoming new examples. In these countries, ethno cultural centrism will cause more conflicts and hinder national integration.

In a multicultural era, media should respect differences and diversity among cultures and function as a method of integration. One country and even one city cannot help having different races and different cultures coexist. The Netherlands and Sweden developed leading multicultural policies and Canada and Australia adopted multiculturalism as the national policy.

The Korean government announced "Comprehensive Countermeasures for Recognition Improvement of Multiculture" in August 2012 and started to improve people's understanding of multicultural society and acceptance of cultural diversity in order to form a tolerant society. Especially, the government distributed teacher's manuals about study management, guidance of life, and consultation for multicultural students. It also began to widely provide multicultural education to government employees, police officers, soldiers, and employees of multicultural institutions. Moreover, it encourages diversity in broadcasting and media. Using broadcasting and cultural contents, it will provide Multicultural Respect Education, develop various programs regarding multiculturalism, and support the budgets of the EBS (Educational Broadcasting System) which will make relevant programs. From 2013, the guidebook for kindergarten teachers and textbooks of elementary, middle, and high school will include contents regarding multiculturalism.

Note:

1 Multicultural families consist of married immigrants, people who acquired Korean citizenship at birth, or foreigners naturalized as Koreans.

References:

Allport, G. W. *The Nature of Prejudice*. Cambridge: Perseus Books, 1954. Print.
Barker, Chris. *Television, Globalization and Cultural Identities*. Buckingham: Open University Press, 1999. Print.
Gerbner, G., L. Gross, M. Morgan, N. Signorielli, and J. Shanahan. *Growing up with Television: The Cultivation Processes*. 2002. Print.
Goff, B. G. and H. W. "Goddard. Terminal core values associated with adolescent problem behaviors." *Adolescence*. 1999. Print.
Held, David and John Thompson. *Social Theory Modern Societies: Anthony Giddens and his Critics*, Cambridge University Press. 1989, Print.
Huntington, P. Samuel. *The Clash of Civilization and the Remaking of World Order*. New York: George Borchardt, 1996. Print.
Kim, Hyun-Joo. "Assimilation of Foreigners in Korea: Focus on Intercultural Communication and Social Networks." *The Korean Society for Journalism & Communication Studies*. 1997. Print.
Lee, Yeon. "The Culture Conflict and Media." *Global Society and Media*. Minervashobo Press (Japan), 2003. Print.
Lee, Yong-Jae. "A Study on the Actual Condition of Information Literacy of Immigrants in Korea." *Korea Library and Science Society*: 2009. Print.
Müller, Harald. *Das Zusammenleben der Kulturen*. Frankfurt am Main: Fischer Taschenbuch Verlag, 1998. Print.
Woo, Hyung-Jin and Joseph R. Dominick. "Acculturation, Cultivation, and Daytime TV Talk Show." *Journalism and Mass Communication Quarterly Vol. 80*: 109–127. Print.
Yang, Hyep-Seung. "The Effect of Interpersonal Communication and Korean Media Consumption on the Perception of Korean Values and on the Attitude toward Korea among Immigrants and Sojourners in Korea." *The Korean Society for Journalism & Communication Studies*. 2011. Print.

Japanese Media and Multicultural Society

Yuga SUZUKI
Sophia University, Japan

1. Introduction
   1–1 Foreigners in Japan: Status & Problems
2. Contemporary Situation
   2–1 Ethnic & Media: Media for Foreigners in Japan
   2–2 Media Environment of Foreigners in Japan
3. Consideration: From Ethnic Media towards Multicultural Media

1. Introduction

Japanese society is often said to be "one race" and a "society lacking diversity." Compared to the examples of Australian society (government) and Canadian society (government) which advocate "multicultural society" and "multiculturalism" as national policy, Japan may in a way compare poorly and have a closed feeling. But in contrast to evaluation of the degree of progress in "civilization" (civilization is advanced, low degree of development), one cannot apply measurement to "culture" (or said another way, some things which are not evaluated by high or low levels with people, aspects and circumstances). Also, the advance of globalization spreads such culture across borders.

Japan does not have media like Australia's Special Broadcasting Service. But since the Great Hanshin Earthquake (1995), starting with emergency broadcasts by multilingual radio stations, multilingual radio and media broadcasts have attracted attention. Also, amidst progress in cable and satellite broadcasts and a move to digital broadcasts, there is an increase in foreign language paid channels such as broadcasts in Chinese, Korean, Portuguese and Tagalog languages.[1] Also, in multilingual broadcast services, Japanese and English language broadcasts are leading, but there is a limited English-speaking population among foreigners in Japan. Looking at another dimension, local government publicity etc. is now commonly multicultural in paper media and using the internet, especially in English, Chinese and Korean languages and so on.[2]

1-1 Foreigners in Japan: Status & Problems

Table1 Number of Registered Foreigners 2014

Country

China	654,777	30.9%
North & South Korea	501,230	23.6%
Philippines	217,585	10.3%
Brazil	175,410	8.3%
Vietnam	99,865	4.7%
USA	51,256	2.4%
Peru	47,978	2.3%
Thailand	43,081	2.0%
Nepal	42,346	2.0%
Taiwan	40,197	1.9%

Others	248,106	11.7%
Total	2,121,831	100.0%

Source: Ministry of Justice "Foreigner Statistics Table"

According to 2014 statistics, there were 2,121,831 registered foreigners, which is less than 2% of Japan's total population, but this is about 60.9% more than 20 years earlier in the year 1994. Anyway, the situation is a long term growth trend after the 2011 Great East Japan Earthquake.

Viewed by nationality (origin), China is top at 650,000 people, comprising 30.9% of the total. This is followed by North and South Korea, Philippines, Brazil, Vietnam and the USA. Viewed by year, China is in a growth trend each year, while North and South Korea are in a decreasing trend. Brazil natives have also been in a decreasing trend since 2008.

On the other hand, about 13,410,000 foreigners entered Japan in 2014; this was 3,050,000 more than the previous year, becoming the largest number in history. 16,900,000 Japanese left Japan in 2014. Looking at statistics for the end of June 2015, the number of foreign residents in Japan reached about 2,543,000. Amidst the rising tide of globalization, not only "things" but also "people" are moving in large numbers on a global scale. Japan's globalization can be seen in the large numbers of foreigners living in Japan and their diverse nationalities.

Looking back on the history of foreigners residing long term in Japan, it goes back more than 150 years to the foreigner residence zones of the late Edo Period. There, many foreign language media (newspapers) were issued by these foreigners. There are roughly two periods of sudden increase in the immigration of foreigners into Japan. People who crossed over from the Korean peninsula from the 1920s to 1930s are called "Old comers" and "Old residents," which brought the appearance of newspapers followed by magazine media. They are distinguished from people called "Newcomers" and "New arrivals" who came since the 1980s.

Path towards Long Term Residence
When World War II ended in 1945, there were about 2 million Koreans in Japan, and about 90,000 Chinese. Of these, about 520,000 Koreans had no choice but to stay in Japan. North and South Koreans in Japan still face ethnic discrimination in their lives in Japan.

Looking back on modern Japanese society, one could say residence became an issue after the Vietnam War ended in 1975. Many refugees fled the neighboring countries of Vietnam, Laos and Cambodia, and some of them wanted to come to Japan. The Japanese government had a negative posture on receiving them, but there was action on long term residence, partly due to international criticism.

In the 1980s, Japanese society experienced export growth and its trade surplus boomed. In this fast economic growth period, the excess rural population moved into urban areas, and economic development brought steady progress in population movements, so foreign laborers were not needed. But in the bubble economy era, there was a stronger tendency among young people to keep away from "difficult, dirty, dangerous" work, so small and medium companies faced the problem of labor shortages involving simple tasks. This caused them to bring foreign workers to Japan, and workers streamed in from the Philippines, Thailand, China, Pakistan, Iran and Bangladesh.

Japanese society accepts specialized engineers, but had a policy of rejecting simple laborers, so there arose debates on whether to adopt an "open country policy" which receives a labor force, or an unchanged traditional "closed country policy."

2. Contemporary Situation

2–1 Ethnic & Media: Media for Foreigners in Japan

Ethnic media is a source of information for foreigners. Ethnic media has various definitions, but this paper defines it as "Information media (publishing, broadcasts, internet, etc.) used relating to their ethnicity, by ethnic minority people who live in that nation" (Shiramizu: 2004). Many foreigners who live in the Japanese nation cannot understand the Japanese language, so this information media is transmitted in their respective mother languages, is used to foster and maintain each ethnic identity, and is needed to protect the rights of ethnic groups in weak positions.

A narrow definition of ethnic media is expressed according to the definition of Lincoln democracy: "Media, of the ethnic group, by the ethnic group, for the ethnic group" (A. Ishi, 2002; Shiramizu, 2004). That is, who the owner is, who it is edited by, and who receives it. Another important issue is, instead of being sent from a foreign country, that it is created in the country of residence, so it would be made in Japan for people in Japan. Recent years have seen Japanese people involved in the creators' side (capital and reporters, etc.), and much ethnic media is issued in Japanese language for the second and later generations.

As mentioned above, ethnic media began in Japan for foreigners who came from foreign countries to Japan from the end of the Edo Period to the Meiji Era; it was published in residence zones where they were specially allowed to live and work. It is an undisputed fact that since the Meiji Era, English language newspapers published by Japanese and foreigners were the leading periodicals in ethnic media. Later, people came from the Korean peninsula and China, thus the numbers and content of ethnic media slowly diversified and increased. Compared to media in that country's language, ethnic media provides newly arrived foreigners with various information in their mother language with no language ability barriers; it greatly helps them to understand such information, and is greatly relied on. Accurate numbers are not available, but around the 1980s there were at least 150 printed media alone published in at least 15 languages.[3]

Since the 1980s, the long term fast economic growth period brought to Japan foreigners "newcomers" who had varied backgrounds: countries of origin, reasons for coming to Japan, family composition, etc. This resulted in the appearance of huge numbers of ethnic media for newcomers. Shiramizu called this period the "Ethnic Media Rush Hour" (Shiramizu: 2004) or "Age of Ethnic Flood." In addition to the previous printed and broadcast media, a system was developed to view contents created outside that country even in Japan for a fee, via the communications satellite PerfecTV. Moreover, geographical spread using the internet (email magazines and web sites, and so on) enabled the expansion of ethnic media.

2–2 Media Environment of Foreigners in Japan

Here, a survey[4] done in March 2010 by NHK Broadcasting Culture Research Institute looked at the media environment of foreigners in Japan, and shows its characteristics. The survey covered media for people from the four countries with the largest number of residents in

Japan (China, Korea, Brazil, Philippines).

Firstly, as shown in Table 1, at least 90% said that the media they usually use is "Japanese language TV," showing a high contact ratio. Except for Brazilians, three countries also have similar high percentages using the internet in the "Japanese language" and "Mother language." Except for Koreans, relatively high percentages have contact with "Mother language newspapers/magazines (free)," but only a low 10% to 25% use "Japanese language newspapers/magazines (paid)" media.

There is not a simple correlation between Japanese language TV use and Japanese language ability. Chinese and Koreans use Japanese language TV more than Brazilians and Filipinos, but "Japanese language TV" and "Internet" are familiar daily media for all foreigners.

However, looking at what kinds of information they get from that TV (Table 2), we see clear differences. Chinese and Koreans get news and information, ranging from in Japan to their native country and the world. But Brazilians and Filipinos get only limited information. Viewed by type, Brazilians like sports, music, animation, children's programs, and so on, more than programs which require Japanese language ability. In contrast, Chinese and Koreans often view documentaries, news, and information programs.

Looking at the media Koreans most commonly use, Japanese language and mother language internet media are used more than Japanese language and mother language TV (see Table 3). Partly because PCs are less common among Brazilians, "newspapers/magazines (paid and free)" comprise a large percentage of their mother language media. One reason for the low percentages viewing mother language TV is because paid transmissions are not cheap.

Table 2: Media Usually Used

MA (%)

	China	Korea	Brazil	Philippines
Japanese language TV	94	90	95	98
Mother language TV	32	17	10	22
English language TV	4	2	0	3
Japanese language newspapers/magazines (paid)	25	17	10	5
Japanese language newspapers/magazines (free)	37	3	9	2
Mother language newspapers/magazines (paid)	1	2	89	52
Mother language newspapers/magazines (free)	50	3	88	100
English language newspapers/magazines (paid/free)	4	4	0	8
Japanese language radio	16	5	3	62
Mother language radio	6	0	3	1
English language radio	2	5	0	12
Japanese language internet	79	92	14	86
Mother language internet	86	92	48	90
English language internet	9	59	8	79

Table 3: Information Obtained from Japanese Language TV

MA (%)

	China	Korea	Brazil	Philippines
Local information about the city/town/village I live in (clothing, medical, food, work, housing, etc.)	24	2	0	4

News and information about the prefecture I live in	40	6	2	3
Information about my fellows and acquaintances who also came from my country	0	0	0	1
News and information about events in Japan	93	75	19	93
Native country news and information	12	10	4	16
News and information about the world other than Japan or my native country	38	70	7	14
Other	9	25	67	3

Related to Japanese ability, looking at Japanese language and mother language internet use, people who access both frequently (among 6 stages, ranging from "Use very little or not at all" to "At least 2 hours daily") are often those "Strong in Japanese language." In contrast, we see that people who access infrequently do not have strong Japanese language skills. This is almost the same as their tendency to access "Mother language internet." Viewed by country, frequency of using "Japanese language internet" is daily (ranging from about 20–30 minutes to at least 2 hours) for 57% of Chinese and 49% of Koreans, while 80% of Filipinos use it about 20–30 minutes.

Regarding Japanese language ability, readers of "Japanese language newspapers and magazines" have strong Japanese language ability, while people with "Not much or almost no" ability have a strong tendency to "Use mother language newspapers and magazines." We found that TV (Japanese language or mother language) is not closely related to Japanese language ability.

The above shows that an "Information divide" in media use also exists among foreigners in Japan, similar to the divide in Japanese society as a whole. Similar to the above-mentioned differences in information from TV (see Table 3), differences are also seen in information obtained from the internet.

As shown in Table 4, from mother language internet, native country news and information are ranked first for most. But Japanese domestic news and information is what were obtained more often from Japanese language internet. However, Chinese and Koreans look at their native country and then the world, while in contrast the residents from the other two countries tend to want to obtain local information.

Table 4 Information Obtained on Internet: Top 3

MA

		First	Second	Third
China & Korea	Mother language internet	Native country news and information	News and information about the world other than Japan or my native country	Information about fellows & acquaintances who also came from my country
	Japanese language internet	News and information on events in Japan	News and information about the world other than Japan or my native country	News and information about the prefecture I live in
Brazil	Mother language internet	Other	Native country news and information	News and information about the world other than Japan or my native country
	Japanese language internet	Other	News and information on events in Japan	Native country news and information
Philippines	Mother language internet	Native country news and information	Other	News and information on events in Japan
	Japanese language internet	News and information on events in Japan	Local information about the city/town/village I live in (clothing, medical, food, work, housing, etc.)	Other

*Question items are same as Table 2

3. Consideration: From Ethnic Media towards Multicultural Media

Ethnic Media plays an important role in the lives of foreigners in Japan. On the other hand, some people fear that its very existence **"impairs coexistence"** with Japanese society. Also, the instability of its information provision is a concern. Ethnic media's information has a limited main aim which is basically information provision to ethnic groups, so it has a closed aspect. Ethnic media and ethnic minorities can become treated in a fixed and substantive way, which in contrast can create fences (isolation, segmentation) between current media and information, and "Invisible Residents" (Kajita, 2005).

Looking at long term residency of foreigners in Japan, especially the characteristics of Brazilians, many belong to the community as an ethnic group of Brazilians, and can use Portuguese language to understand everything in their work and daily lives. They use ethnic media written in Portuguese for lifestyle information etc., so they stick to the Brazilian community, live in a closed community, and their Japanese language ability does not improve. Angelo Ishi also wrote "The Brazilian community relies only on ethnic media as its main information source, which one cannot say is a healthy situation" (2010). This suggests the problem that ethnic media in such a community can be reproduced in a closed, exclusive way.

While they have lifestyle infrastructure in Japan, communication with Japanese people is minimized, and all speech is in Portuguese language in areas with various ethnic businesses for shopping and daily life goods. This creates concerns of conditions in which Japanese people and foreigners do not help each other in society. Shiramizu also points out what he calls the condition of living in a "psychological enclave" (Shiramizu, 2010).

For foreigners living in Japan, ethnic media is a great help for a lifestyle in Japan which is totally different from their native country. Thus it is an essential tool. On the other hand, one cannot deny that its very existence encourages them to be stuck in their separate communities, with all of their living done there. While in Japan, they do not substantially belong to Japan, inviting aspects of segmentation and isolation.

In the above-mentioned NHK survey (2010), "Does Japan's mass media sufficiently communicate about foreigners' opinions and conditions?" received high percentages of negative replies from each country's foreigners: over 80% of Brazilians and over 60% of Filipinos replied "Not communicated much." In addition, regarding "I feel that Japan's mass media has discriminatory reporting, and takes up mistaken images of minorities," relatively high percentages said "Often/sometimes," showing a high 48% of Chinese, and 65% of Koreans, and almost 1/3 of Filipinos answered "Often."

The most common replies regarding requests to NHK were "Native country news and information" (80%, Filipinos), "I want broadcasts of news in simple Japanese language" (78%, Brazilians), "I want the usual news broadcast in my mother language voice or subtitles" (73%, Brazilians).

Therefore, it still may be difficult to say that an environment is arranged for ethnic media to function fully in Japan as a multicultural society. However, NHK World is aimed at overseas, but its live streaming in 18 languages can be viewed in Japan, and podcasting etc. can also be used. Also, terrestrial broadcasts are in both Japanese and English languages, and there are subtitled broadcasts. Soap operas from overseas are mostly made in the U.S., but there are many original language and subtitled programs in both terrestrial and communication satellite broadcasts.

The writer was living in Australia when multilingual experimental broadcasts (radio) began. SBS is in a sense a tool which clearly demonstrates the social role of mass media. This is because the nation advocates multiculturalism, and SBS was established as a public body for this purpose. In that sense, with their origins as public broadcast bodies, it may be significant to compare NHK, ABC and SBS.

In the past 10 years or so, in addition to radio and TV broadcasts, ethnic media has enhanced its functional aspects by actively utilizing internet media. But ethnic press first appeared in the mid-19th century as printed media in mother languages, and passed through a long period of reliance on native country information. Since the introduction of multiculturalism policy in the 1970s, ethnic media has attracted attention. Shiramizu pointed out that it provided (1) group internal functions, (2) inter-group functions, (3) social stability functions,[5] which seems indisputable. But one problem is that a group with a mother language which actually has long broadcast hours (although exceptional) is actually a majority in Australian society, and it does not necessarily serve as a media tool for the minority. This paper discussed "Japanese language" and other "mother languages," but we can replace these terms with "mainstream" and "non-mainstream languages" and consider the meaning of contents.

Amidst the range of optimistic, critical and negative views of multiculturalism, how can we view Australia's SBS which is media unmistakably developed as a tool of national policy? Although Japan is not an immigrant nation, this may be one model to consider for the future of Japan's mass media.

Finally, we look at future research. In the legal system for the broadcast and communications field, comparative research on foreign language broadcasts (multilingual) will be useful. Japan is not advocating a multicultural society, but there are similarities and differences between Australia, Canada, the USA and the UK (or France) in their multicultural and multilingual aspects and the methods of their media initiatives. It may be necessary to compare with a model country of multicultural, multilingual society.

With their historical backgrounds, partly because Koreans and Chinese have long histories of printed media, they already form ethnic majorities. It may be useful to separate these from ethnic minorities, and conduct ethnic media research.

SBS also actively utilizes an interactive site via the internet. It is important to also research differences in contents of conventional and current printed media, broadcasts and net media, and the characteristics of people who use broadcast and net as access media. An interesting issue is residents from North Korea and China who use Japan, where freedom of expression is protected, as a stage to express their views, utilizing newspapers, magazines and cyberspace. In looking at how far the political aspects of the internet (political aspects of content) involve ethnic media and (host country, native country) society, ethnic factors are greater than politics, which may be a research issue which should be focused on.

Notes:

1. Communications satellite Sky PerfecTV has these foreign language broadcasts (excluding English): "TV Globe" and "RECORD International" (Portuguese), "Channel China" and "CCTV Omiya" (Chinese) / "KNTV" (Korean) / "TFC The Filipino Channel" (Tagalog).
2. For example, Hamamatsu City in Shizuoka Prefecture has a population of 820,000. Nearly 4% of them are foreigners, which is much greater than the national average of 1.7%. In particular, Brazilians comprise over half of the registered foreigners. Consequently, there is much publicity in the English and Portuguese languages, and active development of government internet sites (multilingual living information site: Canal Hamamatsu, etc.).
3. Shiramizu 2010, 33.
4. Ritsu Yonekura and Masana Tani "Media Environment and Media Conduct for Foreigners Living in Japan," *Broadcast Research and Survey*, August Edition, 2010, 70–81.
5. Ethnic media's functions can be broadly categorized into group internal functions, inter-group functions, and social stability functions. Group internal functions are for people in the ethnic group, ranging from daily lifestyle information, to information to maintain the ethnic group's ethnicity; this can be divided into (1) Lifestyle information provision function, (2) Psychological group formation function, (3) Entertainment and sublimation function, (4) Local contribution and advocacy function, (5) Public opinion advocacy and enlightenment function, (6) Function of maintaining and handing down one's own culture. The inter-group functions serve as bridge-building between the ethnic group and the greater society for their coexistence, and have the function of linking with fellow groups and the country of origin. The third is social stability functions, providing public information and working to reduce possibilities of opposition and conflict, and providing information which adapts to the environment (Shiramizu 2004, 87–89).

References:

Ang, I., G. Hawkins and L. Dabboussy. *THE SBS STORY: The Challenge of Cultural Diversity*, Sydney: UNSW Press, 2008. Print.

Furuhashi, Yuka. "Creating Information for Coexistence ~ Information Provision from Hamamatsu City Government ~." Diss. Sophia University (Department of Journalism), 2012. Print.

Hawkins, Gay. "The Special Broadcasting Service and Australian Multiculturalism." *Globalization and Media: Australia and Asia*. (Symposium paper for Australian Studies of Japan, Sophia University), May 2010.

Ishi, Angelo. "Public Relations for Foreign Residents in Japan." *International Culture Training*. No. 69 (2010): 22–29. Print.

Kajita, Takamichi, Kiyoto Tanno and Naoto Higuchi. *Invisible Residents*. University of Nagoya Press. 2005. Print.

Sekine, Masami. *Arrival of Multiculturalist Society*. Asahi Sensho. 2000. Print.

Shiramizu, Shigehiko. *Ethnic Media—Aiming at a Multicultural Society Japan*. Akashi Shoten. 1996. Print.

Shiramizu, Shigehiko. *Ethnic Media Research—Cross-border, Multicultural, Identity*. Akashi Shoten. 2004. Print.

Shiramizu, Shigehiko. "New Developments in Ethnic Media." *SJS* (2010): 27–43. Print.

Suzuki, Yuga. "Australia's Broadcasts—Progress of Diversity—Contemporary Situation of SBS." *Journalism & Media*. Nihon University. No. 4 (2011). Print.

Takeda, Isami et al. eds. *Introduction to Australia*, 2nd Edition. University of Tokyo Press. 2007. Print.

Yonekura, Ritsu. "How Should Broadcasts be Arranged for 'Creating a Multicultural Society'①." *Broadcast Research and Surveys*, October Edition. 2009. 56–67. Print.

Yonekura, Ritsu. "How Should Broadcasts be Arranged for 'Creating a Multicultural Society'②." *Broadcast Research and Surveys*, December Edition. 2009. 20–31. Print.

Yonekura, Ritsu and Masana Tani. "Media Environment and Media Conduct for Foreigners Living in Japan." *Broadcast Research and Surveys*, August Edition. 2010. 70–81. Print.

Contributors

Yasue ARIMITSU is Professor Emeritus of English and Australian Studies, Doshisha University, Kyoto, Japan. She is the author of *Finding a Place: Landscape and the Search for Identity in the Early Novels of Patrick White* (1986) and *Australian Identity: Struggle and Transformation in Australian Literature* (2003). She co-authored *An Introduction to Australian Studies, 2nd Edition* (2007). She has also edited and contributed to translating *Diamond Dog: An Anthology of Contemporary Australian Short Stories — Reflections on Multicultural Society* (2008). Her article "Nation and Literature: Literary Possibilities in a Multicultural Society" was published in Wolfgang Zach/ Ulrich Pallua (eds.) *Racism, Slavery, and Literature* (2010). "Nam Le's *The Boat*: A Reflection of Multiple Selves," Michael Kenneally, Rhona Richman Kenneally, and Wolfgang Zach (eds), *Literatures in English: New Ethical, Cultural, and Transnational Perspectives* (2014). She was the president of the Australian Studies Association of Japan (2010–2013), and currently the president of the Australia New Zealand Literary Society of Japan (2014–).

Kate DARIAN-SMITH is Professor of Australian Studies and History, School of Historical and Philosophical Studies, University of Melbourne. She has been the Director of the Australian Centre from 1998, and held several senior positions at the University.

Kate has been the recipient of numerous ARC research grants, and has published several books, book chapters and articles on Australian cultural history and Australian studies, including on war: memory; cultural heritage and museology; colonialism; architectural design; childhood; and has just commenced a new project on visual culture and photojournalism.

She is on the Board of the Australia-Japan Foundation, DFAT, and has been involved with Australian Studies in Europe and Asia for over two decades. She co-edited, with Professor Yasue Arimitsu, the book *Diamond*

Dog: An Anthology of Contemporary Australian Short Stories which Reflect Multicultural Society, Gendai Kikakshitsu Publishers.

Kate served two terms as elected President of the International Association of Australian Studies (InASA). She served on the Council, Australian Museum of Australian Democracy at Old Parliament House; and inaugural Chair, Arts and Heritage Collections Advisory Committee, City of Melbourne.

Yeon LEE, Ph.D. (Journalism, Sophia University, 1991). Professor, Department of Journalism and Mass Communication, Sun Moon University. Successive occupation : President of Institute of International Communication Research. Dean, College of Social Science of Sun Moon University. President of the Korea Partnership for Emergency Warning Forum. Commissioner of Press Arbitration Commission of Korea.Research Field: History of Communication, Crisis Management and Communication, Media Ethics and Law, Mass Culture.Publications: "Press Control in Chosen (2002)," "Crisis Management and Communication (2003)," "Crisis Management and Mass Media (2006)," "Japan Broadcasting and Culture (2006)," "Crisis Management Communication of Governments and Corporations (2010)."

Shiao-Ying SHEN, is Associate Professor in the Department of Foreign Languages and Literature at National Taiwan University. Her writings on cinema have been published in *Chung-Wai Literary Monthly, Tamkang Review, Post Script, Journal of Art Studies,* and *Journal of Chinese Cinemas*, and her papers have been anthologized in different books on Chinese cinemas. She is also co-editor of and contributor to *Passionate Detachment: Films of Hou Hsiao-Hsien* (2000), and *In Light of Cinema and Time: City, History, and Aesthetics in Hou Hsiao-Hsien's Films* (2014).

Yuga SUZUKI, Ph.D. (Journalism, Sophia University, 2001). Professor, Department of Journalism, Faculty of Humanities, Sophia University.

Successive occupation: Chairperson of the Department of Journalism; Dean of the Graduate School of Humanities; Secretary of General for Japan Society for Studies in Journalism and Mass Communication. **Research Field:** Journalism History, International Communication; **Joint-work:** *Korean Media Today* (2012), *Introduction to Australia 2nd ed.* (2007), *Seminar Japanese Mass Media 3rd ed.* (2016), "Information Gap in the Globalization" (*Global Society and Media*, 2003).

Guanglin WANG, Professor of English at Shanghai University of International Business & Economics, and Adjunct Professor at School of Media, Culture and Creative Arts, Faculty of Humanities, Curtin University. He is the author of *Being and Becoming: On Cultural Identities of Diasporic Chinese Writers in America and Australia* (Tianjin: Nankai University Press, 2004, 2006) and a number of papers on English, American and Australian literatures. He co-edited with Professor David Carter, the book *Modern Australian Criticism and Theory* (China Ocean University Press, 2010). He is the chief editor of Contemporary Australian Novels in Chinese Translation, which won special translation award from ACC. He is also the translator of *Walden, Background of European Literature*, *Imagined Human Beings*, *Shanghai Dancing*, and a number of novels by Chinese American writers. He is Vice President of Australian Studies Association of China (2014–), and serves on the editorial board of Anthem Studies in Australian Literature, Anthem Press.

Contemporary Australian Studies
Literature, History, Film and Media Studies in a Globalizing Age
現代オーストラリア研究

2016 年 6 月 15 日　初版発行

編　　者　　有　満　保　江
　　　　　　鈴　木　雄　雅

発 行 者　　山　口　隆　史

印　　刷　　株式会社太平印刷社

発 行 所　　株式会社 音羽書房鶴見書店
〒 113-0033 東京都文京区本郷 4-1-14
TEL　03-3814-0491
FAX　03-3814-9250
URL：http://www.otowatsurumi.com

Printed in Japan
ISBN978-4-7553-0292-3 C3000

© 2016　有満保江、鈴木雄雅
組版・ほんのしろ／装幀・吉成美佐（オセロ）
製本・株式会社太平印刷社